Good Cheap Eats

in London 1995/6

© Harden's Guides, 1995

ISBN 1-873721-07-2

British Library Cataloguing-in-Publication data:
a catalogue record for this book is available from
the British Library.

Printed and bound in Finland by
Werner Söderström Osakeyhtiö.

Harden's Guides
PO Box 1500
London SW5 0DX

Contents

RATINGS

Ratings are based both on our own experiences – we have visited all of the establishments at our own expense – and also on the views of the reporters who take part in our annual survey. We have given ratings as follows:

★★   Worth travelling for
London's top bargains. They offer a quality of cooking which is, at the price, exceptional.

★   Worth remembering
Places where the cooking offers notably good value for money.

𝔸   Good atmosphere
Spots with particular "buzz", style or charm.

PRICES

So you can compare the costs of different establishments, we have tried to give a realistic estimate of the cost for a typical meal in each place.

For *restaurants, pubs and wine bars,* we have given an estimate of the cost for one (1) person of two courses with a drink and a cup of coffee.

For *cafés,* the price we show is the approximate cost of a sandwich, a cake and a cup of coffee.

These prices include service (we have included a 10% tip if there is no service charge), VAT and any cover charge.

* Where an asterisk appears next to the price, you can usually keep expenditure to £20 a head or less only at certain times of day (usually lunch), and eating at other times may be much more expensive – see the text of the entry for details. In the area lists, the ratings for such restaurants appear in brackets, eg *(𝔸 ★)*.

Telephone numbers – only '0181' numbers are prefixed; all others are '0171' numbers.

Map number and reference – shown immediately after the telephone number.

Last orders time – the first entry in the small print (Sunday time may be up to 90 minutes earlier).

Opening times – unless otherwise stated, restaurants are open for lunch and dinner seven days a week.

Credit and charge cards – unless otherwise stated, Mastercard, Visa, Amex and Switch cards are accepted.

Smoking – Restrictions on smoking cigarettes are noted. Pipe and cigar smokers should call ahead to check.

Introduction

This is the second edition of the only annual London restaurant guide which is devoted to eating out on a budget.

The importance of offering good value is gaining ever greater recognition among London restaurateurs, and this year we have been able to increase significantly the range of establishments listed.

Our aim has been to cover the full range of less expensive eating experiences, up to a maximum of £20 per person, for two courses, a drink, a coffee and a tip.

Twenty pounds? Cheap? No, we're not suggesting that a £40 meal for two is a cheap one, and, indeed, most of the places in this book will cost you well below that. And in many cases, the 'formula' price we use – which includes two courses, a drink, a coffee and service – will tend to overstate your likely actual expenditure.

There are a few places, though, where there is no point in pretending that you can spend much less than £20 a head. We've included them because we think that it's part of our job to include those places you might like to consider – perhaps for a celebration or a special treat – even if they are at the top end of what most people would think of as budget dining.

An area we have focused on this year is the bargain meals which are available in some of the best and most glamorous restaurants in town – if you're prepared to have your main meal of the day at 'off-peak' times (usually lunch) there are some superb deals available. Many of the meals which approach the top end of our price-range are in fact such 'bargain' offers at top places.

In the write-ups, we have concentrated on trying to say *why* we think any particular place deserves your attention. Some of the listings, especially the starred ones, are worth actively seeking out – others are included simply because they are handy places to know about in their particular area or are especially suitable for certain types of occasion.

As a purchaser of this book, you have identified yourself as someone to whom dining out well – as well as reasonably economically – is important. As such, we hope that you may wish to take part in our annual summer survey of the London restaurant scene. If you would like to do so, please register by returning the form which is the last page of this book. **If you take part in the survey (to be returned by mid-August) you will receive a complimentary copy of our comprehensive guide, Harden's London Restaurants, published the following October.**

Richard Harden   **Peter Harden**

Top places

Recommendations

Top Food

For £10 a head or less

Brick Lane Beigel Bake (E1)
Café Sofra (W1, WC2)
Churchill (W8)
Diwana Bhel-Poori
  House (NW1)
Dôme (chain, prix-fixe menu only)
Food for Thought (WC2)
Kastoori (SW17)
Lahore Kebab House (E1)
Lisboa Patisserie (W10)
Moshi Moshi Sushi (EC2)

The Place Below (EC2)
Pret A Manger (chain)
Royal China (W2, SW15)
Wagamama (WC1)

For over £10 a head

Adam's Café (W12)
Ajimura (WC2)
Albero & Grana (SW3)
L'Altro (W11)
Bahn Thai (W1)
Bedlington Café (W4)
Benihana (W1, SW3, NW3)
The Brackenbury (W6)
Brasserie St Quentin (SW3)
The Eagle (EC1)
Eco (SW4)
Efes Kebab House (W1)
Fina Estampa (SE1)
Frederick's (N1)
Fung Shing (WC2)
Futures (EC2, EC3)
Geale's (W8)
Gilbert's (SW7)
Granita (N1)
Greek Valley (NW8)
Harbour City (W1)
Ikkyu (W1, WC2)
Kalamaras, Mega (W2)
Kalamaras, Micro (W2)
Kensington Place (W8)
Launceston Place (W8)
Laurent (NW2)
Lou Pescadou (SW5)
Mayflower (W1)
Mon Plaisir (WC2)
Mr Kong (WC2)
Museum St Café (WC1)
Namaste (E1)
Odette's (NW1)

The People's Palace (SE1)
Poons, Lisle Street (WC2)
Poons (WC2)
Rani (N3)
The Red Pepper (W9)
Rules (WC2)
Shaw's (SW7)
Simpson's of Cornhill (EC3)
Snows on the Green (W6)
Sonny's (SW13)
Sri Siam (W1)
Le Suquet (SW3)
Thailand (SE14)
Toff's (N10)
Topsy-Tasty (W4)
Turner's (SW3)
Walton's (SW3)
The Waterloo
  Fire Station (SE1)

Most interesting ethnic places

Adam's Café (W12)
Ajimura (WC2)
Bahn Thai (W1)
Bedlington Café (W4)
Café Sofra (W1, WC2)
Churchill (W8)
Diwana Bhel-Poori
   House (NW1)
Fina Estampa (SE1)
Fung Shing (WC2)
Harbour City (W1)
Ikkyu (W1, WC2)
Inaho (W2)
Kastoori (SW17)

Lahore Kebab House (E1)
Laurent (NW2)
Mayflower (W1)
Moshi Moshi Sushi (EC2)
Mr Kong (WC2)
Namaste (E1)
Poons (WC2)
Poons, Lisle Street (WC2)
Rani (N3)
Royal China (W2, SW15)
Sri Siam (W1)
Thailand (SE14)
Topsy-Tasty (W4)
Wagamama (WC1)

Special deals at top restaurants

Benihana (W1, SW3, NW3)
Brasserie St Quentin (SW3)
Chutney Mary (SW10)
English Garden (SW3)
English House (SW3)
Frederick's (N1)
Gilbert's (SW7)
Granita (N1)
Kensington Place (W8)
Launceston Place (W8)
Lindsay House (W1)
Lou Pescadou (SW5)

Maggie Jones's (W8)
Mon Plaisir (WC2)
Odette's (NW1)
Quaglino's (W1)
Rules (WC2)
Shaw's (SW7)
Simpsons-in-
   the-Strand (WC2)
Snows on the Green (W6)
Le Suquet (SW3)
Turner's (SW3)
Walton's (SW3)

Top romantic recommendations

A Tavola (NW8)
Andrew Edmunds (W1)
Anglo Asian Tandoori (N16)
The Ark (W8)
Battersea Barge
   Bistro (SW8)
Bleeding Heart (EC1)
La Bouchée (SW7)
Boudin Blanc (W1)
Brahms (SW1)
Brasserie St Quentin (SW3)
Byron's (NW3)
Café Bohème (W1)
La Cage Imaginaire (NW3)
English Garden (SW3)
English House (SW3)
La Fenice (W11)
Frederick's (N1)
Frocks (E9)

Kalamaras, Mega (W2)
Kettners (W1)
Launceston Place (W8)
Lindsay House (W1)
Maggie Jones's (W8)
Mars (WC2)
Le Mercury (N1)
Mon Petit Plaisir (W8)
Mon Plaisir (WC2)
Odette's (NW1)
Pélican (WC2)
Rules (WC2)
Shaw's (SW7)
Tate Gallery (SW1)
Thierry's (SW3)
Turner's (SW3)
Walton's (SW3)
Yum Yum (N16)

Recommendations

The best fun places

Albero & Grana (SW3)
Banners (N8)
Bar Gansa (NW1)
Bar Madrid (W1)
La Bouchée (SW7)
Boudin Blanc (W1)
Café Pacifico (WC2)
Casale Franco (N1)
Da Mario (SW7)
Dixie's Bar & Grill (SW11)
Down Mexico Way (W1)
Eco (SW4)
Efes Kebab House (W1)
Formula Veneta (SW10)
El Gaucho (SW3)
Hard Rock Café (W1)
Hoults (SW17)
House on
  Rosslyn Hill (NW3)
Jim Thompson's (SW6)
Joe's Brasserie (SW6)
Kettners (W1)
Khan's (W2)
Lemonia (NW1)
Mars (WC2)
Meson Doña Ana (W11)
Mongolian Barbecue
Naked Turtle (SW14)
Osteria Basilico (W11)
Pitcher & Piano (W1, WC2)
Pizza Pomodoro (SW3)
Planet Hollywood (W1)
Pucci Pizza (SW3)
Rock Island Diner (W1)
Ruby in the
  Dust (N1, NW1, SW11)
Rueda (SW4)
Shillibeer's (N7)
The Ship (SW18)
606 Club (SW10)
Sticky Fingers (W8)
Sydney Street Café (SW3)
Texas Embassy
  Cantina (WC2)
Texas Lone Star (SW7)
Thai Pot (WC2)
The Waterloo
  Fire Station (SE1)

The most stylish places

Albero & Grana (SW3)
Bar Central (SW3)
Basil St Hotel (SW3)
Belgo Noord (NW1)
Ben's Thai (W9)
Bibendum
  Oyster Bar (SW3)
Brasserie St Quentin (SW3)
Café de Colombia
  Museum of Mankind (W1)
Café dell'Ugo (SE1)
Café Lazeez (SW7)
City Brasserie (EC3)
Claridges Causerie (W1)
The Criterion (W1)
De Cecco (SW6)
La Delizia (SW3, SW5)
Down Mexico Way (W1)
Eco (SW4)
English Garden (SW3)
English House (SW3)
La Fenice (W11)
The Fifth Floor
  Harvey Nichols (SW1)
Formula Veneta (SW10)
Frederick's (N1)
Kensington Place (W8)
Kettners (W1)
Launceston Place (W8)
Lindsay House (W1)
Mas Café (W11)
Odette's (NW1)
Le Palais du Jardin (WC2)
Pélican (WC2)
The People's Palace (SE1)
Pizza On The Park (SW1)
Poons (WC2)
Quaglino's (W1)
Rules (WC2)
Shaw's (SW7)
Simpsons-in-
  the-Strand (WC2)
Soho Soho (W1)
Sonny's (SW13)
The Stepping Stone (SW8)
Le Suquet (SW3)
Tate Gallery (SW1)
Wagamama (WC1)
Waldorf Hotel (WC2)
Walton's (SW3)
Wilson's (W14)
ZeNW3 (NW3)

Directory

A Tavola NW8   £18   A
7 St John's Wood High St   586 4776   7-3A   1

*A very enjoyable, relaxed atmosphere is the chief draw to this
recently established, rustically decorated St John's Wood
Italian, which has already carved out a loyal following. In our
experience, the pasta (£5 to £7) is not as good as you might
hope, but if you stick to the buffet of antipasti (£5.90 or
£7.90) and the puddings, you can have an enjoyable meal at
reasonable cost. House wines are £10.50 and £12, which,
however good they are, seems rather OTT for an
establishment of this type.* / 10.45 pm; no credit cards.

Adam's Café W12   £14   A★★
77 Askew Rd   0181-743 0572   1-3A   2

*By day, it's just a 'greasy Joe', but at night this family-run
Shepherd's Bush café transforms itself into a popular,
atmospheric Tunisian café. The couscous is excellent, with the
most expensive choice being the Royale (£7.95). There is also
a small selection of grilled fish and grilled meat skewers at a
similar price. The house wine is £6.95, or you can BYO for
55p per person corkage. The front room is nicer than the
newer rear annex.* / 11 pm; D only; closed Sun; no credit cards.

Ajimura WC2   £19*   ★★
51-53 Shelton St   240 9424   3-2C   3

*Tucked away on the fringes of Covent Garden, this
unassuming place – Britain's oldest Japanese restaurant –
serves high quality, good value food. Pick carefully and you
can eat quite inexpensively even from the à la carte menu,
but the set meals are particularly worth remembering. The
set lunches (£8 to £9) include miso soup, rice, pickles and a
main dish. The pre-theatre set dinners (£13 to £14.50),
served between 6pm and 7.30pm also include sashimi.
A bottle of Kirin beer is £2.40.* / 10.30 pm; closed Sat L & Sun;
no Switch; no smoking area.

Alba EC1   £17   ★
107 Whitecross St   588 1798   8-1B   4

*Success has brought expansion to this sparsely decorated
restaurant cum wine-bar – one of the few decent eating
places near the Barbican. The modern Italian cooking
(specialising in dishes from Piedmont) is notably good, and
can be enjoyed economically by sticking to the simpler dishes
and excellent pastas. You might follow a salad of artichokes
with gruyère and parmesan (£5.50), with a risotto combining
pepper sausage, leeks and celery (£5.90). House wine is
some £9 a bottle.* / 11 pm; closed Sat & Sun.

Albero & Grana SW3 £ 16 A ★★
89 Sloane Ave 225 1048 4-2C 5
The most stylish tapas bar in town is also one of the best, and it's perhaps unsurprising – especially given the place's trendy Brompton Cross location – that it's often packed with a fashionable crowd. Most of the dishes are in the £4 to £6 price range – for example Spanish sausage with chick-peas (£3.80), mixed paella (£5.25), garlic chicken (£6) – and you can, despite house wine at £10 a bottle, have an enjoyable, light meal at a relatively reasonable cost. / 11 pm.

Ali Baba NW1 £ 11 ★
32 Ivor Pl 723 5805 7-4A 6
Lost in a backwater off the north end of Baker Street, this quirky, family run restaurant (entered through a take-away) is a good place for high quality, yet inexpensive Middle Eastern dishes – particularly Egyptian specialities. Starters are about £2, and main dishes about £5. Unlicensed – you can BYO with no corkage. English is certainly not the first language here. / Midnight; no credit cards.

All Saints W11 £ 19 A ★
12 All Saints Rd 243 2808 5-1B 7
This ultra laid-back Notting Hill café – on the street which used to be London's most notorious for drug dealing – is one of the top, cool Portobello hang-outs. It's particularly well-known for its affordable weekend brunch, when a full cooked breakfast is about £4 and pasta dishes under £6. With reasonable care, you could also dine here within budget. From a changing menu strong on salads and fish dishes, you might have bruschetta (£3.50) to start, followed by vegetable curry with coconut rice (£8.25). House wine is £8.50. Not a place to go if you're in a hurry. / 11.30 pm; D only Mon, closed Sun D; no Amex.

L'Altro W11 £14* ★★
210 Kensington Pk Rd 792 1066 5-1A 8
At night, this is a fashionable and very expensive Italian fish restaurant. At lunchtime, though, they offer a range of high quality tapas-type dishes at very reasonable cost (£3 to £5), making the place relatively affordable and, at that time of day, possibly the best value choice in Notting Hill's trendy restaurant strip. House wine is £8.90. / 11 pm; closed Sun D.

Andrew Edmunds W1 £ 15 A ★
46 Lexington St 437 5708 2-2C 9
If only there were more restaurants like this candle-lit Soho townhouse, which not only offers bags of atmosphere for your money, but also imaginative, very enjoyable, simple modern British dishes. You might follow escabeche of fennel and field mushrooms (£3.95), with Italian sausages and basil mash (£5.95). The house wine is £8.50, and there's an unusually good range at only marginally higher cost. Book. / 10.45 pm.

Anglo Asian Tandoori N16 £14 𝔸
60-62 Stoke Newington Ch St 254 9298 1-*1C* 10
*This low-lit restaurant in Stoke Newington offers good,
standard Indian dishes in, what is, for the area, an unusually
comfortable and atmospheric setting. Tandoori dishes are the
speciality (for example the mixed grill, including rice and nan
for £7.25), and they do all the standard curries (around £3).
Cobra is £2.95 for a large bottle. / Midnight, Fri & Sat 1 am;
no smoking area.*

Archduke Wine Bar SE1 £10 𝔸
Arch 153, Concert Hall Appr. 928 9370 2-3D 11
*It will be interesting to see if the opening of the People's
Palace, in the nearby South Bank Centre, has any effect on
the standards offered by this well known wine bar/restaurant
(characterfully located beneath railway arches). As things
stand, there's little wrong with the wine bar staples such as
quiche and salad (£3.95) or the hot dishes of the day
(£4.95), but no one could really accuse them of offering much
in the way of culinary excitement either. Best value is the
£10.95 'menu presto' of two courses and coffee, offered in
the restaurant at lunch and from 5.30pm to 7.30pm.
House wine is £8.75. / 11 pm; closed Sat L & Sun.*

The Ark W8 £17 𝔸
122 Palace Gdns Ter 229 4024 5-2B 12
*For over thirty years, this Alpine chalet, somehow mislocated
just off Notting Hill Gate, has dispensed undemanding
franglais fare in cosy surroundings, and it remains an
enjoyable place for a relaxing supper. Typical dishes are
moules marinières (£3.90) or onion soup (£2.50) to start,
with rack of lamb (£8.75) or baked cod (£7.90) for a main
course. There are also two and three course set lunches for
£7.50 and £9.75. House wine is £7.80. / 11.15 pm;
closed Sat L & Sun.*

Arts Theatre Café WC2 £18 ★
6-7 Gt Newport St 497 8014 3-3B 13
*Some people really take to this odd, rather seedy basement
restaurant – which doubles as the bar of the theatre upstairs.
At the price, it offers unusually ambitious Mediterranean
cooking. There is always a soup (at £3.50), a pasta dish
(at £7.50) and the main courses, say braised lamb, are priced
in the £8 to £10 range. There is a three course menu
(£12.50), but it offers a very restricted choice. House wine
is £8.50. / 11 pm; closed Sat L & Sun; no credit cards.*

Aykoku-Kaku EC4   £ 15   ★
9 Walbrook   248 2548   8-3C   14
This large Japanese basement restaurant is situated just behind the Mansion House. At dinner if offers no budget options, but it is a popular City lunching venue on account of its good value set meals (offered only in a restricted area of the restaurant). These cost between £8 and £13 (depending upon the main dish), and include an hors d'oeuvre, miso soup, rice, pickles, salad and fruit as well as the main item. Kirin beer is £2.90 a bottle. / 10 pm; closed Sat & Sun; no booking for inexpensive lunches.

Bahn Thai W1   £ 19   ★★
21a Frith St   437 8504   3-2A   15
The quality of its cooking makes this Soho spot one of the best known of the central Thai restaurants. The menu is unusually wide-ranging, including wild boar, frogs' legs and venison. Leaving aside the more exotic items, prices for starters are around £4 to £6 and most main courses are around £7.50. Singha beer is £2.75 a bottle. / 11.15 pm.

Bangkok SW7   £ 14   ★
9 Bute St   584 8529   4-2B   16
The menu of the longest established Thai restaurant in the UK induces a feeling of comfortable certainty. It never changes, but nor does the standard of the cooking, and the place's cosy, canteen-like premises attract a steady local following and a constant stream of visitors. Soups are a little over £3, while a typical main dish would be chicken with basil and chilli (£5.70). Singha beer is £2.30. / 11 pm; closed Sun; no Amex.

Banners N8   £ 13   𝔸
21 Park Rd   0181-348 2930   1-1C   17
The laid-back atmosphere is the great attraction of this mellow café/bar/restaurant in Crouch End (where, to satisfy licensing regulations, you must have food with alcohol). The cooking is not exciting, but there's a wide choice through the day, starting with a breakfast fry-up (£5.75), and including dishes as diverse as burgers and Indian stew (both £6.75). House wine is £8.95 a litre and beers range from Newcastle Brown (£2) to Erdinger Pikantus (£3.10). / 11.30 pm.

Bar Central   £ 18   𝔸★
316 King's Rd, SW3   352 0025   4-3C   18
131 Waterloo Rd, SE1   928 5086   8-4A   19
The newly opened King's Road branch of this expanding chain is the more expensive of their two current outlets. You could easily spend over our budget there, but if you stick with main dishes such as pizza (£6 to £7) or risotto (£7.50), it is not too hard to stay within it. At Waterloo, although they do not do pizza, everything is a little less pricey. You could start with soup (£3.50) followed by Cuban-style hamburger (£5.50) or steak sandwich (£7.50). House wine is £9 in Chelsea, £8 in Waterloo. / 11.45 pm; no Amex.

Bar Gansa NW1   £13   A★
20
2 Inverness St   267 8909   7-3B

Even people who don't like tapas bars sometimes really take to this buzzing younger scene place in Camden Town. The tapas range from garlic bread with tomato, or green beans with garlic (both £1.95) up to more substantial dishes such as grilled marinated prawns (£3.50), or minute steak with chips (£6.95). A bottle of house wine is £7.50. / 11.30 pm; no Amex & no Switch.

Bar Italia W1   £4   A
21
22 Frith St   437 4520   3-2A

Famously open practically all hours (23 out of 24, seven days a week), this Soho coffee shop has been a fixture for over forty years. The snacks are run-of-the-mill, but the coffee is pretty good and – despite growing local competition – the place remains the number one social centre for the early hours demi-monde. Unlicensed. / 6 am; no credit cards; no booking.

Bar Madrid W1   £12   A
22
4 Winsley St   436 4649   2-2B

One of the less tacky singles scenes in London is to be found at this loud 'n' lively bar north of Oxford Street. The place stops short of being a full-blown night club, though there is a small dance-floor and an entrance fee which varies (depending on when you go) from nil to £5 for women and £3 to £7 for men. The food is, of course, pretty much incidental, but the tapas (£1.75 to £2.95) are perfectly OK. House wine is £7.85 a bottle. / Viva Brazil 2.30 am, Bar Madrid 2.30 am; D only; closed Sun; no Switch.

Barcelona Tapas Bar E1   £13   ★
23
1a Bell Ln   247 7014   8-2D

This basic basement bar, off Petticoat Lane market, has established itself as an unlikely retreat for City gents wanting an interesting and not too expensive lunch. Choose your tapas – from olives (£1) to Mediterranean prawns (£6.50) – from the extensive range displayed under the glass-topped counter. House wine is £7.50. / 10.30 pm; closed Sat & Sun D; no booking.

Basil St Hotel SW3   £19*   A
24
8 Basil St   581 3311   4-1D

If Knightsbridge is getting on your nerves, retreat by at least half a century to the creakily charming dining room of this family-owned hotel. You can, within our price range, enjoy a visit here for the set lunch (£13.95 for two courses, with house wine at £9.95). The hotel also does afternoon teas which, at £5.95 for the cream tea or £9.25 for the full afternoon tea, offer very good value. / 9.45 pm; closed Sat L.

Battersea Barge Bistro SW8   £14   A
Nine Elms Ln   498 0004   6-1D   25

If you can find this old barge (despite the name, it's moored in Vauxhall, down a lane opposite New Covent Garden Market), it makes a charming and unusual venue for a riverside meal (especially on a warm evening) or for a party. The unambitious food is not, frankly, a particular attraction, but it is no reason not to go and it is inexpensive — for example, salad Niçoise (£2), fillet of pork Normande (£6.50), desserts (£1.50). House wine is £6.50. / 11 pm; closed Sun; no credit cards.

Bedlington Café W4   £11   ★★
24 Fauconberg Rd   0181-994 1965   1-3A   26

A distant location has done absolutely nothing to dim the fame of this Chiswick 'greasy Joe', which, by night, becomes one of London's best Thai restaurants. The place is not much to look at (though, as we go to press, improvements are scheduled), but the dishes are spicy, generous and very reasonably priced — few main courses are over £4 and many are under £3. BYO — 50p corkage per person. / 10 pm; no credit cards.

Belgo Noord NW1   £17   A★
72 Chalk Farm Rd   267 0718   7-2B   27

Everyone should go at least once to this extraordinary, stylish refectory, whose fame has spread far beyond its Camden Town home. The short, Belgian-inspired menu focuses mainly on mussels done in many different ways (£7.95 to £8.95), accompanied by a huge selection of flavoured Belgian beers (most popular is Hoegaarden, £2.25 per half pint). Set deals are a constantly changing feature of the menu — at the time of writing they include the lunchtime Psycho-kilo (a kilo of moules, chips and a beer for £5) and the evening 'Beat the Clock' (eat three courses between 6pm and 8pm and pay between £6 and £8 depending on when you finish). It's a shame, given these good value offerings, to load on a 15% service charge — justifiable, if ever, only in the grandest places. (An offshoot, Belgo Centraal — to be two or three times as big as the original — is opening as we go to press. It's at 50 Earlham Street, WC2 (tel 813 2233), and, if it lives up to expectations, will be one of the most striking newcomers of 1995.) / 11.30 pm.

Ben's Thai W9   £12   A★
93 Warrington Cr   266 3134   7-4A   28

It's very well worth the journey to the airy Thai dining room above this huge Maida Vale pub (the Warrington Hotel) — one of the best all-round budget eateries in town. Surroundings are much above average, and the inexpensive menu (starters are about £2.50, main dishes £4 to £5, and a bottle of beer £2.20) is consistently realised to a high standard. It is sensible to book. / 10.30 pm; D only; no Amex & no Switch.

Café Bohème W1   **£ 18**   A★
13 Old Compton St   734 0623   3-2A   50

*For once, a place that lives up to its name – you can just go
for a coffee, and it is quite bohemian. That's not the end of
the attractions, though, for its mainly young and trendy Soho
following. They like the fact that you can go all day (from
8am) and much of the night (till 3am – restricted menu after
midnight), and that you can have a well cooked light dish –
such as pasta (£5.50), moules marinières (£4.75) or a
burger (£5.80) or (pushing our price limit) something more
substantial. House wine is £8.50.* / 2.45 am.

**Café de Colombia
Museum of Mankind W1**   **£ 14**   A★
6 Burlington Gdns   287 8148   2-2B   51

*When you've had enough of window-shopping in the
Burlington Arcade, restore the spirits with a visit to this
fashionable café, hidden away within the Museum of
Mankind. Salads are the thing here – perhaps with grilled
chicken or couscous, all priced around £6 and £7 – and also
cakes (£3) and a range of Colombian coffee (there is no tea).
House wine is £9.95.* / L only, Sun pm cakes only; no smoking;
no booking.

Café de la Place SW11   **£ 16**   A★
11/12 Battersea Sq   978 5374   6-1C   52

*This Battersea establishment – more a classic local bistro
than a café – offers not particularly polished, but thoroughly
enjoyable real cooking at very reasonable prices. A la carte,
you might choose crab soup, (£3.25) followed by maigret of
duck (£8.95), but they also offer a set three course lunch or
dinner for £9.99 (say pâté, beef stroganoff and chocolate
mousse). House wine is £8.45.* / 10.30 pm; closed Sun D; no Amex.

Café Delancey NW1   **£ 18**   A★
3 Delancey St   387 1985   7-3B   53

*This large, popular, all-day Camden Town standby is really a
brasserie rather than a café. The full menu is served all day
long, and if you want a Delancey breakfast (£5.35, including
coffee) at dinner-time, no one will mind. This makes it a
particularly popular weekend brunch spot (no booking).
Typical of the menu are chicken liver salad (£4.75), croque
monsieur (£3.95) and steak sandwich (£6.75), though one
or two more substantial dishes are available. The house wine
is £8.50.* / 11.45 pm; no Amex.

Café dell'Ugo SE1 £14 A★
                                         54
56-58 Tooley St   407 6001   8-4C
*A location in the arches beneath London Bridge (near the
London Dungeon) may not sound particularly attractive,
but this modishly decorated spot has established a solid
reputation for interesting cooking (modern British with a
Moroccan twist). The restaurant is borderline so far as our
budget is concerned, but the bar offers light dishes like deep
fried calamari (£3.95), Caesar salad (£4.75) and rump steak
on ciabatta (£5.95). House wine in the bar is £7.95. / 11 pm;
closed Sat L & Sun.*

Café Fish (Wine Bar) SW1 £13 ★
                                         55
39 Panton St   930 3999   3-4A
*For a quick, tasty snack in Theatreland at a reasonable price,
this hot and rather cramped cellar offers a reliable standby.
The menu is mainly familiar fish dishes – moules marinières
(£4.25), crab sandwich (£4.40), fish pie (£5.25) – plus a few
items for carnivores. House wine is £7.75. / 11.30 pm;
closed Sat L & Sun; no Switch; no smoking area.*

Café Grove W11 £10 A
                                         56
253 Portobello Rd   243 1094   5-1A
*On a sunny Saturday, when trendy bohemians, visitors and
mere shoppers gravitate to the Portobello Road, the large
terrace of this Notting Hill café becomes the number one
vantage point from which to watch the world go by – you may
well have to queue for a place. The fare – omelettes (£3 to
£5), salads (about £6) and cakes (£1.70) – has no particular
aspirations. On summer nights, the café is open. In previous
years they have gone Mexican, but the style for this year is
undecided as we go to press. / 6 pm, summer later; summer,
closed Sat D & Sun D; no credit cards; no booking.*

Café Lazeez SW7 £18 A★
                                         57
93-95 Old Brompton Rd   581 9993   4-2C
*The crisp, modern style of this South Kensington
café/restaurant is shared by few other Indian restaurants in
London. It is one of the few which could be called fashionable
and the 'evolved' cuisine it offers is enjoyed by many who do
not usually like Indian cooking. At night, the full menu includes
a number of fairly expensive dishes, but it is not too difficult
to eat quite cheaply. By day, there is also a café menu
(chicken salad Lazeez at £5.95 typifies the style) and they
do a set two course lunch for £7.50. On Sundays, there is
an £8.95 buffet. The wine list is much broader than usual,
or you can drink Cobra or Grolsch at £3 a bottle. / 12.30 am,
Sun 10.30 pm; no smoking area.*

Café Météor W6 £14 A★
158 Fulham Palace Rd   0181-741 5037   6-1A 58

Despite its slightly obscure location opposite the Charing
Cross Hospital – which, visitors please note, is actually in
Hammersmith – this casual brasserie has quite a wide
reputation as a reasonably priced destination. Dishes it offers
– mostly bistro staples – include fish soup (£3.75), croque
monsieur (£4.50) and grey mullet with fries (£8.50). There is
also a bar menu with items such as cheeseburgers (£5.95)
or smoked chicken salad (£4.95). On Wednesdays, they have
live music. House wine is £7.95 and the Météor beer from
Alsace is £1.55. / 10.45 pm; no smoking area.

Café Montpeliano SW3 £13 ★
144 Brompton Rd   225 2926   4-1C 59

If you want to join the Knightsbridge ladies who lunch, or just
need a shopping break from Harrods (on the other side of
the road), this quite glamorous all-day café/brasserie offers a
reliable and – for this bit of town – pretty economical option.
A typical starter would be bruschetta (£3.50), followed
perhaps by pastas (around a fiver) or chicken (£7.95).
There is a large selection of cakes for £2.50. House wine
is £6.50. / 11 pm; closed Sun D; no Switch; book only for L

Café Pacifico WC2 £18 A
5 Langley St   379 7728   3-2C 60

The main attraction of this Covent Garden cantina is that it's
one of the most atmospheric and buzzing American places in
London. Like most London Mexicans, the food's not much to
shout about, though Margueritas (£3.95) at the bar while you
wait – there is no booking – will dull your tastebuds anyway. A
dish like nachos Pacifico to start is £3.95 and the main dishes
– enchiladas, burritos, chimichangas, and so on –
are mostly £7 to £8. Tecate is £2.50 a bottle. / 11.45 pm;
no smoking area; book pre 6.30 pm only.

Café Sofra £8 A★★
10 Shepherd's Mkt, W1   495 3434   2-3B 61
1 Bow St, WC2   240 9995   3-3D 62

For 365 days a year, these stylish cafés – offshoots of the
well-reputed and expanding Sofra chain – offer good value,
often delicious Middle Eastern snacks (falafel, filled pitta
bread, salads, etc) and good pastries. Mousakka (at £3.50) is
the most expensive dish on the menu. For £3 they offer a
selection of meze. Both cafés are unlicensed but you can BYO.
No cheques are accepted. / Midnight; no credit cards; no booking.

Café Tabac SW15   **£12**   A
30 Putney High Rd   0181-788 8668   6-2B   63
The food at this Putney bistro (right by the bridge) is not going
to set the world on fire, but, if you are looking for a real meal,
relatively inexpensively, it offers some reliable options.
The hungry should consider the five course set menu – for
only £9.75, you might have crudités, smoked salmon roulade,
stuffed saddle of lamb, cheese, and chocolate supreme.
There is also a mere three course option for £7.50, and at
lunch a three course deal for £4.75 – typically, crudités, leg of
lamb and a pudding. House wine is £7.95. / 11 pm; closed Sun D;
no Amex & no Switch.

Caffe Graffiti NW3   **£18**   A
71 High Street   431 7579   7-2A   64
This brightly lit, welcoming, modern restaurant in the middle
of Hampstead looks as if it might be all top swank and offer
little in the way of culinary excitement. It's true that the dishes
such as marinated chicken salad (£3.95) or lamb fillet
(£8.95) are not hugely ambitious, but they are in fact very
competently cooked. At lunchtime, there's a two course set
menu for £8. The house wine is £8.25. / 11 pm; no Amex.

La Cage Imaginaire NW3   **£15**   A★
16 Flask Wk   794 6674   7-1A   65
A visit to this French restaurant in a Hampstead backwater
can be a highly enjoyable experience – it's a pretty little place,
with good food. It is possible, with care, to keep within our
price range in the evening – much easier at lunch when you
can enjoy three courses (perhaps sautéed prawns, followed
by guinea fowl with crêpe suzette to finish) for £9.95.
House wine is £8.50. / 11 pm, Sat 11.30 pm; closed Mon; no Switch.

Calabash WC2   **£14**   –
38 King St   836 1976   3-3C   66
Covent Garden may seem an unlikely location for a safari, but
the pan-continental menu of the restaurant in the bowels of
the Africa Centre permits you to voyage far and wide, without
ever leaving London. A typical starter would be fried plantain
(£2.30) and for a main dish you might try groundnut stew
with peanut butter (£6.25) or couscous with lamb (£7.50).
There are a number of African wines (from £7.50), and South
African beer has finally appeared on the menu, in the form
of Castle (at £2 a bottle). The setting is rather musty, but
benefits from extra authenticity when drums echo through the
centre at the weekends. / 10.30 pm; closed Sat L & Sun; no Switch.

Calzone   **£11**   A★
2a Kensington Pk Rd, W11   243 2003   5-2B   67
66 Heath St, NW3   794 6775   7-1A   68
These stylish, slightly hard-edged pizzerias in Notting Hill and
Hampstead offer a pretty consistent formula of good quality
pizzas (from £4.75 to £5.75) and other light dishes, such as
the house salad (£5.75) and a selection of pastas (£4.95).
House wine is £7.95. A new Fulham Road branch is opening
during 1995. / 11.30 pm; W11 no Amex.

Camden Brasserie NW1   £19   A★
216 Camden High St   482 2114   7-2B   69
*It may not really be a brasserie (they aren't open all day),
but this recently refurbished and expanded establishment is
one of north London's more consistent success stories.
Traditionally, the speciality has been grills (burger and
chips, £6.25), but of late their menu has taken on a slightly
Mediterranean flavour, with the addition of pastas (around
£6) and more substantial dishes. House wine is £9.25.*
/ 11.30 pm; no Amex.

Caravan Serai W1   £16   A★
50 Paddington St   935 1208   2-1A   70
*London's only Afghani restaurant (the cuisine is a cross
between Indian and Persian), situated just off Marylebone
High Street, is a cosy place decorated with rugs. At night,
you might choose fried aubergine (£3.95) followed by lamb
cooked with spinach (£5.25) – the most expensive main dish
is prawns (at £9). At lunch they offer a very good value, three
course meal, where there is quite a good degree of choice for
£9.95 (coffee included). House wine is quite
pricey at £9.95.* / 11 pm, Fri & Sat 11.30 pm; no Switch; no smoking area.

Carnevale EC1   £12   ★
135 Whitecross St   250 3452   8-1B   71
*This tiny but smart vegetarian restaurant north of the
Barbican is now open in the evenings, making it ideal before a
play or a concert – as there's not much else round about, it
would be a good idea to book. You can start the day off here
with a good range of pastries. Later on, they offer two course
(£8.50) and three course (£10.50) set menus, featuring a
range of interesting dishes – for example chilled chervil soup,
saffron risotto, or rocket salad with new potatoes and
mushrooms. The house wine is £9.* / 10.30 pm; closed Sat & Sun;
no credit cards.

Casale Franco N1   £19   A★
134-137 Upper St   226 8994   7-3D   72
*This Italian restaurant in Islington may be hidden away
down an alley, but its fame attracts a wide following, and
there's often a queue (no booking, except at lunch).
Grilled vegetables (£4.50) is one of the most popular starters.
The pizzas (£6.20 to £8.50) are among the best in town,
but this isn't a pizzeria in the normal sense, and you can't
have one on its own after 8pm. If you order a non-pizza
main course, you could easily spend over our limit. House
wine is £9.* / 11.30 pm; closed Mon, D only Tue-Thu; no Amex;
no smoking area; no booking.

Chaba SW10 £16 ★
206 Fulham Rd   352 8664   4-3B 73
This unpretentious Thai basement restaurant on the fringe of Chelsea, can easily be overlooked amidst the competing attractions of its brasher neighbours. It's worth seeking it out, though, if you're looking for carefully cooked dishes (mostly around a fiver) and a warm welcome. A bottle of Singha beer is £2.20. / 11.30 pm; closed Sat L; no Switch.

Chelsea Bun Diner SW10 £8 ★
9a Lamont Rd   352 3635   4-3B 74
For a hearty but economical meal in the environs of Chelsea, this bright but rather smoky diner is one of the few places which can be recommended. Kick off the day, from 7am, with a good all-day breakfast (£3.25, but £2.30 before 10am Mon-Fri), or, later on, satisfying international dishes such as avocado salad (£3.35) or Florida Skins (a chicken, cheese and potato skins special, £5.80). The fact that it's strictly a BYO place keeps costs down too. / 11.30 pm; no credit cards.

Chelsea Kitchen SW3 £7 ★
98 King's Rd   589 1330   4-2D 75
In the heart of fashionable Chelsea, the spirit of '60s London still lives at this basic international bistro, whose keen prices still attract the locals as much as passing tourists. The menu, the style of cooking and the décor have survived pretty much unchanged, and, though they charge a fraction more now, you can still get a set three course menu all day for about a fiver – you might have soup, lasagne and sponge pudding. Eating à la carte is only a fraction more expensive. House wine is a mere £5. / 11.45 pm; no credit cards.

Chiang Mai W1 £16 ★
48 Frith St   437 7444   3-2A 76
The quality of the Thai cooking at this Soho restaurant is among the best in the centre of town. The menu focuses on northern Thai specialities (most main courses costing £5 to £7.50) and there is a large vegetarian menu. Thai beer is £2.50. Service here can be excessively leisurely. / 11 pm; closed Sun L; no Switch.

Chicago Pizza Pie Factory W1 £13 –
17 Hanover Sq   629 2669   2-2B 77
They claim to have served Europe's first deep-pan pizzas at this large Mayfair basement in 1977. The place retains a certain degree of period charm, and its prime attraction now (especially for those with kids) is probably as a refuge from Oxford Street. Pizzas are still the mainstay of the menu, but they have also introduced a wide selection of pastas (both types of dishes generally around £6). There are now two and three course lunchtime deals priced at £5.95 and £6.95 respectively, aimed at those who want to eat quickly. House wine is £8.50. / 11.30 pm, Fri & Sat 1 am; no smoking area.

China Court W1 £14 ★
Wardour St   434 0108   3-4A 78
*At the rear of the Swiss Centre, this large Chinese restaurant,
on the fringe of Chinatown, offers high quality cooking in
rather anonymous comfort. At lunchtime, they have a good
range of dim sum (priced from £1.50), while from the main
menu most dishes are priced between £4.90 and £7.50.
A bottle of Tsing Tao beer is £1.95. / 11.30 pm; no Switch.*

Chuen Cheng Ku W1 £14 –
17 Wardour St   437 1398   3-3A 79
*Lunchtime dim sum (from £1.75) – served from a battery of
trolleys – are the most famous attraction at this large, gaudy
Chinatown landmark. In the evening, the fare – with main
courses costing £6.40 and up – is pretty commonplace.
A bottle of Tsing Tao beer is £1.90. / 11.45 pm.*

Churchill W8 £9 𝔸★★
119 Kensington Ch St   792 1246   5-2B 80
*The cheerful Thai annex to this otherwise unremarkable
Notting Hill pub is one of the best known and most popular
super-budget places in west London, so it's always best to
book ahead. They offer a selection of tasty and filling
main dishes (there are no starters) all priced around £5.
House wine is £7.45. / 9.30 pm; closed Sun D; no Amex & no Switch.*

Chutney Mary SW10 £15* ★
535 King's Rd   351 3113   4-4B 81
*This Chelsea Anglo-Indian restaurant aims to recreate the
style of cuisine evolved by the British in India. A smart place
(if a mite themed), it offers a couple of set deals worth
remembering. At lunch or after 10pm you can have a two
course (£10) or three course (£12.95) set meal – perhaps
samosas, minted tandoori chicken tikka and a choice of
desserts – and on Sundays, there is an eat-all-you-can buffet
for £13.95. House wine is £9.75. / 11.30 pm; no smoking area.*

Chutneys NW1 £9 ★
124 Drummond St   388 0604   7-4C 82
*To fill up for under a tenner, it's difficult to beat this plain but
pleasant, vegetarian restaurant in the 'little India' a couple of
minutes' walk from Euston station. At lunchtime and all day
Sunday (for which there is no booking) there is a £3.95
buffet, and in the evening a deluxe thali (three courses,
including rice, popadoms and raita) will set you back only
£5.95. Kingfisher lager is £1.50. / 11.30 pm; no Amex & no Switch.*

City Brasserie EC3 £17* 𝔸
Plantation Hs, Mincing Ln   220 7094   8-3D 83
*The large, glamorous restaurant here is one of the nicest in
the City and well outside our price-bracket. However, for a
civilised light meal, you might like to consider relaxing in the
comfortably furnished lounge area with a club sandwich
(£7.25) or cold poached chicken (£6.50). House wine
is £11.50. / 9 pm; closed Sat & Sun; no Switch; no booking in bar.*

Claridges Causerie W1 £19[*] Ⓐ
Brook St 629 8860 2-2B **84**

It may seem rather odd that visiting royalty's favourite Mayfair hotel should figure in this book. However, you can have a main course (the smörgasbord or the hot dish of the day) and a pudding in the Causerie for £18.50. The price includes a glass of wine. Nurse it – the house wine is priced at £17.50 per bottle. Gentlemen must wear a jacket and tie. / 11 pm; closed Sat D & Sun; no Switch.

Clifton E1 £14 ★
126 Brick Ln 247 2364 1-2D **85**

On this East End street famous for its curry-houses, this once smartly appointed, now somewhat worn, establishment is one of the best-known places. Prices are not that cheap, but the cooking is spicy and well above average. Most main courses are £4 to £5, with the menu featuring one or two unusual dishes such as brain masala (£4.95). To cash in on the current craze, balti are also available (£2.95 to £6.95) both here and at a glossy new offshoot opened next door. A bottle of Kingfisher is £1.60. / 1 am.

Coates EC2 £10 ★
45 London Wall 256 5148 8-2C **86**

For an informal City lunch (or for a meal before a visit to the Barbican), you can do very much worse than this quite comfortable pizzeria, which is decked out in late '80s industrial chic style. Pizzas are £4.40 to £5.95, or you might choose mozzarella and tuna salad or salade Niçoise (both £5.60). The house wine is £7.50. / Mon-Wed 9.30 pm, Thu & Fri 10.30 pm; closed Sat & Sun; no smoking area.

Como Lario SW1 £19 Ⓐ
22 Holbein Pl 730 2954 4-2D **87**

It may be cheap only by the standards of its area, but this elegant, if tightly packed, trattoria a couple of minutes from Sloane Square has long been known as a haven of reasonable value in that expensive part of town. You might have soup (say, thick bean soup with pasta £3.55) followed by pasta (practically all £5.25), a risotto (about £6), or a dish such as breast of chicken (£6.55 – vegetables another £2). House wine is £8.25 per bottle. / 11.30 pm; closed Sun.

F Cooke & Sons E8 £5 –
41 Kingsland High St 254 2878 1-1C **88**

If you are looking for a truly East End experience, invest in a tube ticket to Dalston and visit this, the most famous of pie and eel shops. Eels and mash in liquor (£2.08, £2.91, or £3.62, depending on the size of your appetite and on your nausea threshold) is very much an acquired taste. But even if it turns out that you can't bear the food (in case of emergency, steak and kidney pie is £1.25), the place's turn-of-the-century tiled interior provides some consolation, and the total cost of the visit will not be great. BYO, or tea is 45p a cup. / Mon-Wed 7 pm, Thu 8 pm, Fri & Sat 10 pm; closed Sun; no credit cards; no booking.

Coopers Arms SW3   £11   A★
87 Flood St   376 3120   4-3C   89
This bare but fashionable Chelsea back street pub offers fare
of diverse inspiration, and far above usual pub standards.
Sunday lunch (two courses for £8.50, three courses for £10),
for example, will probably offer the option of unusually well
done traditional dishes – perhaps chicken and chipolata
sausages followed by fruit crumble – as well as some more
obviously fashionable choices. There's a pretty good selection
of wines, or drink Young's bitter at £1.65 a pint. / L only;
closed Sat D & Sun D; book Sun L only.

Cork & Bottle WC2   £14   A★
44-46 Cranbourn St   734 7807   3-3B   90
The West End's most popular wine bar for more than two
decades continues to pack 'em in – don't count on a seat –
to its rather unlikely basement premises, beside a Leicester
Square sex shop. Don't go expecting rock-bottom prices – the
least expensive dish is mushroom pâté (£3.25), the priciest a
steak sandwich (£8.95) – but the cooking is solidly good.
The wines are likewise (the patron being a noted
connoisseur), with the house selection being priced
at £9.95. / Midnight.

Cosmo NW3   £16   ★
4 Northways Pde, Finchley Rd   722 1398   7-2A   91
Displaced both in time (from the '60s) and space (from
somewhere in central Europe), this South Hampstead café
and dining room offers solid, reliable international dishes
(with German specialities). The café always affords the
possibility of a filling meal within our budget (especially
popular for breakfast, when a fry-up is about £3). For a little
more comfort, you can dine in the restaurant (Monday to
Thursday nights) from the three course set menu for £12.95,
or you can have a three course lunch there on weekdays for
£7.25. House wine is £4.95 for a half-litre carafe.
/ 10.45 pm; no Switch.

Costa's Grill W8   £9   ★
12-14 Hillgate St   229 3794   5-2B   92
Claiming to be the oldest Greek restaurant in London (1949),
this rather worn place just south of Notting Hill Gate has
been known to successive generations of west Londoners for
its combination of solid quality and value. The owners can
seem a little bit set in their ways, but, given the moderate
prices – calamari (£1.50), taramasalata (£1.50), kleftiko (£5)
– few people seem to be complaining. House wine is £6.50.
/ 10.30 pm; closed Sun; no credit cards.

Cranks   **£11**   ★

23 Barrett St, W1	495 1340	2-2A	93
8 Marshall St, W1	437 9431	2-2B	94
9 Tottenham St, W1	631 3912	2-1C	95
1 The Market, WC2	379 6508	3-3D	96
17 Great Newport St, WC2	836 5226	3-3B	97
Unit 11, 8 Adelaide St, WC2	836 0660	3-4C	98
5 Cowcross St, EC1	490 4870	8-1A	99

This all-day chain of vegetarian cafeterias offers pretty good overall value and has made attempts of late to brings itself up to date. Every day, they offer two soups (£2.30), one of which is vegan. Main dishes are all about £4 – you might have a Mediterranean grilled vegetable tart or spicy noodles with stir-fried vegetables. If you're in the market for a pot of tea (90p) and a carrot cake (£1.15), these are pleasant places for a short stop-over. House wine is £6.45 (but note that Adelaide St and Cowcross St are not licensed). Cranks are in the process of moving their Covent Garden branch – the new outlet is to be a three storey 'flagship' for the chain. / 7 pm - 10 pm; credit cards - varies by branch; no smoking; no booking.

The Criterion W1   **£17**   𝔸
Piccadilly Circus   925 0909   2-2C   100

Few would dispute that this vast, gilded, neo-Byzantine chamber is the most spectacular dining-room in London. The food is bound to be something of an anticlimax – and it is. However, the £10 two course Mediterranean menu (perhaps rigatoni and aubergine in a cream sauce followed by fried plaice) offers pretty fair value, especially for somewhere so central – the entrance is right by Eros. Afternoon tea (£7.50) and Sunday brunch (where the specials like eggs Benedict are all priced at £5 to £6), are also possibilities worth considering. House wine is £9.50. / 11.30 pm; closed Sun D; no smoking area.

Crown & Goose NW1   **£12**   𝔸★
100 Arlington Rd   485 2342   7-3B   101

This trendified pub in Camden Town offers a reliable standby for sound cooking at reasonable prices, perhaps soup of the day (£2.85) or spicy chicken salad (£4.50), followed by pasta of the day (£4.95) or baked peppers (£5.50). A bottle of the house wine is £7. / 10 pm; closed Fri D; no credit cards.

Czech Club NW6   **£12**   ★
74 West End Ln   372 5251   1-1B   102

If you like the idea of unadorned, traditional mitteleuropean cooking in atmospherically faded surroundings, the restaurant at this friendly West Hampstead émigrés club is for you. Starters, like vegetable soup or Czech sausage, are all £2 to £3, while the main courses are £6.40 to £8.50 – you might choose smoked pork with dumplings, or roast duck. There's a surprisingly good, and reasonably priced, wine list (house wine is £4.50 for half a litre), but why not avail yourself of one of the few opportunities to drink draft Budvar at £1.80 a pint. / 10 pm; closed Mon (ex bank hols) Sat D & Sun D; no credit cards.

Da Mario SW7   £18   Ⓐ
103
15 Gloucester Rd   584 9078   4-1B
In a city curiously short of cheap 'n' cheerful party places, the large dine 'n' disco basement of this PizzaExpress, not far from Hyde Park, is a well known attraction. For downstairs, you must book and choose one of the set menus, of which the cheapest at £16 per head includes garlic bread, pizza or pasta, and half a bottle of wine. / Midnight; no Switch; book for disco.

Da Pierino SW7   £10   –
104
37 Thurloe Pl   581 3770   4-2C
If you're looking for a filling, no-nonsense Italian meal, this friendly, family-run diner in South Kensington has a lot to recommend it. It's not a place where they stand on ceremony – a TV blares in the corner – making it a place kids' antics are more likely to be met with a smile than a scowl. The menu consists of fairly substantial pizzas and pastas and dishes of the day, mostly in the £5 to £7 price-range. House wine is £7.20. / 11.15 pm; closed Mon; no Amex.

Daphne NW1   £13   ★
105
83 Bayham St   267 7322   7-3C
One of Camden Town's (and therefore London's) best and longest established Greek tavernas. Many people opt for the three course meze (£8.75), in addition to which all you would need is bread at 40p a time and house wine at £8.90 a litre. At lunch, they also have two course and three course set meals for £5.75 and £7.50 respectively. There is a large outside terrace open in summer. / 11.30 pm; closed Sun; no Amex & no Switch.

Daquise SW7   £10   Ⓐ
106
20 Thurloe St   589 6117   4-2C
A much-loved South Kensington institution ideally located for visitors to the museums, this Polish café/restaurant has a wonderful ambience, evoking how – we imagine – Warsaw felt in the '50s. The food is authentic – ie not the main attraction – but prices for dishes such as stuffed cabbage (£4.50) are not unduly demanding. It's an all-day place and very popular for tea and (fairly ordinary) cakes (£1 to £1.60). House wine is £6.50. / 11 pm; no credit cards.

De Cecco SW6   £17   Ⓐ★
107
189 New King's Rd   736 1145   6-1B
This buzzing Parson's Green trattoria was voted best budget restaurant in the survey for our companion publication, Harden's London Restaurants. With dishes such as char-grilled vegetables (£4.95), marinated sword fish (£5.50), and spaghetti with clams (£6.50), it's possible to eat well within our price limit, but you could spend quite a lot more if you tried. House wine is £7.50. / 11 pm; closed Sun.

La Delizia £14 A★
63-65 Chelsea Manor St, SW3   376 4111   4-3C 108
Farmers Mkt, Sydney St, SW3   351 6701   4-3C 109
246 Old Brompton Rd, SW5   373 6085   4-2A 110
These Chelsea pizzerias offer thin crust pizzas
(around £6) of consistently high quality, together with a small
range of other dishes (including what is possibly London's best
tiramisu). Their premises all possess a considerable degree of
chic, providing some justification, perhaps, for prices which
are on the high side – house wine is £8.90. On a sunny day,
the outdoor tables of the Farmer's Market branch attract all
of London's young and beautiful, and the service slows down
accordingly. / 11.30 pm-Midnight; no credit cards.

The Depot SW14 £15 A
Mortlake High St   0181-878 9462   6-1A 111
The level of culinary achievement at this large, relaxed Barnes
diner may be nothing special, but its charming riverside
position (with some delightful views, if you get the right table)
ensures a full house on a sunny day. Pastas (about £6) or a
prawn stir-fry (£7.80) typify the menu, and locals say that the
dish of the day is often the best bet. The house wine is £8.
/ 11 pm.

Diwana Bhel-Poori House NW1 £ 8 ★★
121 Drummond St   387 5556   7-3C 112
If you are looking for a really satisfying budget meal, check
out this long-established Indian vegetarian restaurant, a
couple of minutes from Euston station. The eat-all-you-can
buffet lunch is £3.95, but even in the evening you'd be hard
put to spend much more than a tenner. Main dishes such as
the deluxe dosa are £4.30, but many people stick to the
excellent poori after which the place is named (£2.10).
They are unlicensed – BYO, no corkage. / 11.30 pm; no Switch.

Dixie's Bar & Grill SW11 £11 A★
25 Battersea Rs   228 7984   6-2C 113
Success is bringing expansion to this small but rightly popular
Tex/Mex diner in Clapham. It offers all the standard items –
burgers (£4.50), fajitas (£5.50), vegetarian chimichangas
(£4.70) – and at a high and consistent quality level. A bottle
of Rolling Rock to wash them down is £1.95. A good place for
weekend brunch. / 11.30 pm; no Switch.

Dôme £14 A★

38 Long Acre, WC2 379 8650 3-2C *114*
354 King's Rd, SW3 352 2828 4-3B *115*
Kensington Ct, W8 937 6655 4-1A *116*
341 Upper St, N1 226 3414 7-3D *117*
38 High St, NW3 435 4240 7-1A *118*
91 High St, SW19 0181-947 9559 6-2B *119*

At the time of writing, we reckon the three course £4.95 menu available at all Dômes at all times is one of the best value deals available in London. A meal just before going to press offered: a choice of seafood soup or liver pâté; pork chop with cherry sauce, or herring wrapped in bacon; and pear tart or fruit salad. You do not expect high art at this price but everything was of a decent quality and the portions quite generous. The surroundings are well done and attract quite a hip crowd. The only 'catch' is that, if you stray from the set menu, prices rise significantly (though you could still eat well within budget). Drinks prices are no special bargain either – a bottle of the house wine is £7.95 – a bottle of Budvar £2.25. / 10.30 pm – 11 pm; some no Amex; no booking.

Don Pepe NW8 £13 A★

99 Frampton St 262 3834 7-4A *120*

The oldest tapas bar in London, near Edgware Road tube, maintains its lively, welcoming atmosphere. In the bar, most of the dishes are between £2 and £4 and the house wine is £7. There's a restaurant too, which is generally rather less fun and more expensive. At Sunday lunch, either in the restaurant or the bar, you can have a three course meal for £12.50. You might have hors d'oeuvres, paella and a choice of cakes from the trolley. / Midnight, Sat 12.30 am; closed Sun D.

Dove W6 £8 A

19 Upper Mall 0181-748 5405 1-3A *121*

Unsurprisingly, the best pub on the nicest stretch of the river at Hammersmith is a pretty popular place, and, at peak times, you will do very well to get a seat. They offer simple hot dishes, a Sunday roast and, in the evening, one-plate Thai specials – all for around a fiver or a fraction more. London Pride is £1.86 a pint. / 10 pm; closed Fri D and Sat D; no credit cards; no booking.

Down Mexico Way W1 £15 A

25 Swallow St 437 9895 2-2B *122*

In the '20s, this Mayfair address (very near Piccadilly Circus) was London's grandest Spanish restaurant. Its tiled interior survives (indeed, it's a listed monument) and now provides an extremely characterful setting for one of London's most attractive Mexicans. The food – nachos (£3.50), burritos (£7.95), fajitas (£9.95) – doesn't necessarily live up to the rest of the experience, but the place's other virtues make it one of the leading central party venues. The atmospheric bar hosts a Latin disco on Thursday, Friday and Saturday nights (for which they make a £5 entrance charge). / 11.45 pm, Sun 10.30 pm.

Dragon Inn W1 £11 ★
12 Gerrard St 494 0870 3-3A [123]

If you really want to experience quintessential Chinatown, you could do much worse than this rather seedy spot, whose Cantonese cooking is consistently above average. There's a long menu with a great variety of dishes, all moderately priced, and at lunch time you can have dim sum at about £1.50 a piece. Tsing Tao beer is £2. / 11.45 pm, Fri & Sat 12.00 am.

The Eagle EC1 £14 ★★
159 Farringdon Rd 837 1353 8-1A [124]

The first and still the best known of the pubs to be converted into quality eating places continues to draw a wide-ranging clientele to its premises on the northern fringe of the City. Soups and salads are £3.30, pastas £6.50, and fish and meat dishes £7 to £9. With such good Californian/Mediterranean dishes so reasonably priced, it can often be quite a crush, and you may well have difficulty finding a seat. Still, there's quite a jolly atmosphere, helped along by house wine at £7.90. / 10.30 pm; closed Sat & Sun; no credit cards; no booking.

Ebury Street Wine Bar SW1 £17 Ⓐ
139 Ebury St 730 5447 2-4B [125]

This dependable Belgravia wine bar (not far from Victoria station) has long attracted a loyal following by offering good value (if not exactly innovative) cooking, friendly service and a good atmosphere. Typical of the menu are dishes such as smoked trout mousse (£4.45), bangers and mash (£7.45) and chicken breast (£7.95). House wine is £8.50, and there's a fair range of wines by the glass. / 10.30 pm; no Switch.

Eco SW4 £11 Ⓐ★★
162 Clapham High St 978 1108 6-2D [126]

The trendiest, and quite possibly the best pizzeria in town. Its undulating plywood and plaster-decorated premises seem rather out of place in downtown Clapham, but it attracts a wide (and often quite groovy) following. Pizzas are priced between £3.70 and £6 and house wine is £6.50. / 11 pm; Mon-Fri only, no smoking area.

Ed's Easy Diner £9 –
12 Moor St, W1 439 1955 3-2A [127]
362 King's Rd, SW3 352 1956 4-3C [128]
16 Hampstead High St, NW3 431 1958 7-1A [129]

Convincingly designed on a '50s-fantasy theme, these well-known burger-bars are situated in all the trendiest parts of town – Soho, Chelsea and Hampstead. Though not, of late, seeming quite as consistent as used to be the case, they can still be a good place for a quick burger (£3.95) and beer (£2.10). If you prefer something lighter, you might have a California cobb salad (£4.75). Breakfast – a silver dollar pancake (£1.95), for example – is served on weekend mornings (not Soho). / Midnight, Fri & Sat 1 am; no Amex; no booking.

Efes Kebab House   £14   A★★
1) 80 Great Titchfield St, W1   636 1953   2-1B   130
2) 175-177 Gt Portland St, W1   436 0600   2-1B   131
*These large, long-established Turkish restaurants, a little way
north of Oxford Street, offer some of the best and most
reliable value in town. Their appeal stretches from besuited
businessmen to parties. Both places have a good atmosphere,
with Efes I being darker and more characterful, and Efes II
being flashier, and boasting nightly belly-dancing. For a party,
you can take one of the £14 set menus, washed down by
house wine at £7.90 a litre, or, just for a filling dinner, you
might choose a special mixed kebab with rice and salad
(£7.30). / 11.30 pm; I closed Sun.*

Emile's   £18   ★
144 Wandsworth Br Rd, SW6   736 2418   6-1B   132
96-98 Felsham Rd, SW15   0181-789 3323   6-2B   133
*London could do with more reasonably priced local
Anglo/French bistros like these establishments in Fulham and
Putney. No one would describe them as wildly exciting places,
but they do offer fair value, especially from the three course,
£13.50 blackboard menu – you might choose salmon
and crab fishcakes, char-grilled lamb and hot treacle tart.
House wine is £7.50. / 11 pm; D only; closed Sun; no Amex & no Switch.*

The Engineer NW1   £14   A★
65 Gloucester Ave   722 0950   7-3B   134
*This Primrose Hill pub has shot to instant local popularity in
its new incarnation as a trendy bar/restaurant – you can eat
in either section, though the latter is more comfortable.
They serve a shortish selection of well executed, simple dishes
– antipasti (£4), fishcakes (£5.50) and organic rump steak
with baker chips (£9) are typical. House wine is £8. / 11.30 pm;
closed Tue L; no Amex.*

English Garden SW3   £20*   A★
10 Lincoln St   584 7272   4-2D   135
*A similar concept to its sibling, The English House (see next),
and with similar menus and prices, but with a slightly more
obviously restaurant-like setting. The place benefits from a
large conservatory. / 11.15 pm; no Switch.*

English House SW3   £20*   A★
3 Milner St   584 3002   4-2D   136
*London boasts surprisingly few restaurants decorated in a
cutely traditional domestic style. This intimate and discreet
townhouse, hidden away in the heart of fashionable Chelsea,
is one of them. At dinner time, prices here are way out of our
range (and, on a purely culinary level, are difficult to justify),
but, at £14.75, the three course lunch here – perhaps
mushroom and sage tart, pan fried fillet of lemon sole with
green lentils, and chocolate ginger thins – represents good
value, especially as coffee is included. House wine is £9.50.
/ 11.15 pm; no Switch.*

Il Falconiere SW7   **£ 18**   ★
84 Old Brompton Rd   589 2401   4-2B   137
*This traditional-style South Kensington trattoria (not far from
the tube) is one of the more reasonably priced establishments
of its type in fashionable south west London. You can always
eat here within our price range – perhaps insalata Caprese
(£4), with breast of chicken (£6.50) and vegetables (£2.50) –
but the best value is to be had from the two course lunch
for £10. House wine is £8.50.* / 11.45 pm; closed Sun.

Fat Boy's W4   **£ 11**   A ★
10a Edensor Rd   0181-994 8089   6-1A   138
*This Chiswick establishment – English caff by day, Thai café
by night – invites comparison with the well known Bedlington
Café. The cooking is a little less intense here, but similarly low
in price, and the less cramped, mellower atmosphere has
helped the place achieve instant popularity (even if the staff
can be very brusque). Most main dishes are £4 to £5,
and house wine is some £7 – or you can BYO at £1
per head corkage.* / 11 pm; D only; no credit cards.

La Fenice W11   **£ 16**   A
148 Holland Pk Ave   221 6090   5-2A   139
*By the standards of fashionable Italian restaurants, the prices
of this opulently olde worlde Holland Park spot are notably
reasonable, and, even if the food is far short of remarkable,
the overall level of value is really quite impressive. Even if you
go à la carte, with prices such as £2.95 for minestrone, £4.60
for pastas and £7.50 for suprême of chicken, it's really quite
easy to keep within our range. There is also a two course set
lunch for £9.75. The house wine is £7.95.* / 10.45 pm; closed Mon
& Sat L; no Switch.

The Fifth Floor, Harvey Nichols SW1 £20   A ★
Knightsbridge   235 5250   4-1D   140
*As you might expect, prices at this flashy foodie complex
(restaurant, bar, café and shop) above the fashionable
department store are hardly bargain basement. However, the
café (with its views over Knightsbridge) is undoubtedly one of
the most stylish places in London for a light meal – perhaps
fusilli with mussels, chives and saffron (£7.50) followed by
butter pecan ice cream (£3.75) – and, if you go on Monday
night, wine comes at the retail prices charged by the in-house
shop. Otherwise, house wine is £9.75. There is
jazz nightly.* / 10.30 pm; closed Sun; .

Fileric   **£ 4**   ★
57 Old Brompton Rd, SW7   584 2967   4-2C   141
12 Queenstown Rd, SW8   720 4844   6-1C   142
*These unpretentious pâtisseries in South Kensington and
Battersea are useful all-day places for a cup of coffee and a
croissant, or a light dish such as a croque monsieur.
Everything is of a high standard, and few things cost more
than a couple of pounds. The concept and the staff are very
Gallic – and at the South Ken branch, the customers
are likewise.* / no booking.

Fina Estampa SE1 £16 ★★
218 Tower Br Rd   403 1342   8-4D 143
Try to book ahead for an excellent Peruvian meal, served in
the unlikely surroundings of the first floor dining room of a
rather shabby pub by Tower Bridge. If you don't book, you
may have to settle for undistinguished, standard pub staples,
which are also available. South American dishes include
ceviche (£5.50) and lamb in coriander sauce (£7.50), and
there is a three course meal with coffee for £14.95.
House wine is £7.50, or Peru Gold beer is £2 a bottle.
/ 10.45 pm; closed Mon & Sun D; no Switch.

La Finca £14 𝔸
96-98 Pentonville Rd, N1   837 5387   7-3D 144
185 Kennington Ln, SE11   735 1061   6-1D 145
These large, woody tapas bars are both located in areas
(Kennington, and just north of Kings Cross) where they're
pretty much the only show in town – agreeable relaxed places
for a few tapas (£1.95 to £3.90) and a bottle of the house
wine (£7.80). Perhaps surprisingly, they are recommended for
people with kids in tow. Above the Islington branch, there's
quite a nice Latin bar/night-club, Bar Tiempo, for which there
is a £3 entry charge if you are dining (up to £6 if not).
/ 11.30 pm, N1 Fri & Sat 1.30 am.

Food for Thought WC2 £9 ★★
31 Neal St   836 0239   3-2C 146
This very cramped Covent Garden basement offers some of
the best, and best value, vegetarian food in town, and it's a
popular place with shoppers and local office workers.
A typical meal might be walnut soup (£1.90) with coconut
and coriander bread (35p), followed by mushroom pie
(£2.80). It's worth leaving space for a pudding like banana
and strawberry scrunch (£1.90). No smoking – just as well as
it's so cramped. BYO (no corkage). / 7.45 pm, Sun 3.45 pm;
no credit cards; no smoking; no booking.

Formula Veneta SW10 £19 𝔸★
14 Hollywood Rd   352 7612   4-3B 147
One of Chelsea's better and more stylish trattorias (serving
traditional fare with a modern twist), and especially popular
with a younger crowd. With care, you can eat here within our
price limit at any time, but especially at lunch, when there is a
set two course meal for £9.95, including coffee. You might
choose leek lasagne followed by a lamb skewer with
vegetables or a salad. On Sunday, they offer three courses
with coffee for £12.95. House wine is £9.95. / 11.30 pm;
closed Sun D.

Fortnum's Fountain W1 £16 🄰
181 Piccadilly   734 8040   2-2B *148*
*Piccadilly's famous food store boasts a well known, all-day
snackery (with its own entrance in Jermyn Street, for the
evenings). It's a spot popular with locals and visitors for light
dishes like Welsh rarebit (£5.95) or avocado and bacon salad
(£4.50), and especially popular for afternoon tea (£8.50) –
you may have to queue. If you want to treat yourself to an
ice-cream (£3.25), this is probably the most civilised place in
London to do so. House wine is a very reasonable £5.95.
/ Midnight; closed Sun; book only after 6 pm.*

Fox & Anchor EC1 £10* ★
115 Charterhouse St   253 4838   8-1B *149*
*One of the very best possible starts to the day (full English
breakfast, £6.50, from 7am) is to be had at this famous pub
near the Smithfield meat market, and – thanks to the relaxed
local licensing laws – you can wash it down with a pint of
bitter (£1.60). At lunchtime, there is a more expensive grill
menu – an 8oz fillet steak is £8 (plus £1 for veg, £1.25 for
chips), with starters and puddings both about £2.
/ Bkfast & L only; closed Sat L (but open Sat bkfast) & Sun.*

Foxtrot Oscar SW3 £17 🄰
79 Royal Hospital Rd   352 7179   4-3D *150*
*If you want to live the gossip-column life on the cheap, hang
out for a while at this long-established nobs' bistro in the
fashionable heart of Chelsea, near the Royal Hospital.
The atmosphere is a greater attraction than the realisation
of staple dishes such as cottage pie, double eggs Benedict
(both £5.75), or club sandwich (£5.25). House wine weighs
in at £9.75. / 11.30 pm.*

Francofill SW7 £11 ★
1 Old Brompton Rd   584 0087   4-2C *151*
*This plain but handsome dining room, just by South
Kensington station, concentrates on providing a short, light
snack-menu – onion soup (£1.95), croque monsieur (£2.95),
salads (£1.50), lemon tart (£2.50) – consistently competently.
There are also hot dishes of the day for around a fiver. As the
name suggests, this is a place for a pitstop, not an evening.
House wine is £7.95. / 11 pm; no smoking area; no booking.*

Frederick's N1 £19* 🄰★★
106 Camden Pas   359 2888   7-3D *152*
*The largest quality restaurant in Islington is a well-known local
institution. Though the place gets a slightly mixed press, there
is no doubting the value of the set meals. These include a
fixed-price three course dinner at £16.50 (service included),
or the same menu (if you're out by 7.45pm) for £12.50. A
two course weekday lunch menu is £10, and the three course
Sunday lunch £12.50. A typical meal might be brie and pear
tart, followed by noisettes of lamb in pastry, with amaretti
and mascarpone torte to finish. House wine
is £9.95. / 11.30 pm; closed Sun; no smoking area.*

Frocks E9   **£ 16**   A ★
95 Lauriston Rd   0181-986 3161   1-1D   153
This friendly, candle-lit English bistro near Victoria Park is a
beacon in the East End – if there are any other non-ethnic
restaurants worth a visit thereabouts, news of them has yet
to reach us. At night, it's best to book – that option is not
available for the popular weekend all-day breakfasts
(most dishes under £5). At other times, starters (such as
chicken stuffed with ginger mousse) are about £4 and main
dishes (perhaps fish cassoulet) are about £8 to £9.
For weekday lunches there's a two course £9.50 menu.
House wine is £7.50. / 11 pm; closed Sun D; no booking Sun.

Front Page SW3   **£ 12**   A ★
35 Old Church St   352 2908   4-3C   154
A cheerful, clubby, panelled pub, hidden away in an
Old Chelsea backstreet – one of the more charming and
civilised places of its type. The menu is much longer than
average with a selection of dishes, such as hot chicken salad
(£5.70), generally prepared to a high standard. A pint of
Boddingtons is £1.90 or a bottle of house wine £8. / 10 pm;
no Amex & no Switch; no booking.

Fung Shing WC2   **£ 18**   ★ ★
15 Lisle St   437 1539   3-3A   155
For some time, this unremarkable-looking establishment just
north of Leicester Square was reputed to offer the best
Cantonese cooking in London. While it has perhaps lost a
touch of this golden glow, it still offers a very high level of
cooking in neutral surroundings which are quite comfortable
by Chinatown standards. It is not a particularly cheap place –
most main dishes are £6.50 to £9.50 – but still a must for
anyone with a real interest in Chinese cooking. A bottle of
Tsing Tao beer is £2.50. / 11.30 pm.

Futures   **£ 12**   ★ ★
2 Exchange Sq, EC2   638 6341   8-1D   156
8 Botolph Alley, EC3   623 4529   8-3C   157
The original Futures, a take-away in the lanes near the
Monument, is well known in that corner of the City for
providing vegetarian dishes – spicy tomato soup (£1.65),
coconut curry (£3.25) – so good that you don't notice that
they haven't got any meat in them. A glossy new branch has
recently been opened in Broadgate, where you can eat in.
We haven't yet visited, but suspect that the cooking there –
including more substantial dishes such as nut roast or Thai
stir-fry (both £6.25) – will be pretty good too. Breakfast, for
example porridge with milk and honey (£1.80 eat-in, £1.15
take out) is an attraction at both establishments. House wine
is £7.95. / EC3 L only, EC2 10 pm; closed Sat & Sun; EC2, no credit cards.

Gaby's WC2   **£ 8**   ★
30 Charing Cross Rd   836 4233   3-3B   158
This small, '60s (very '60s) diner and take-away near
Leicester Square is known for the value of its salt beef
sandwiches (£4.30, with salad), and its range of quality
Middle Eastern dishes (around £5). House wine is £7.50.
You wouldn't really take people here to impress, but if you just
want a filling pre/post-theatre snack, you'd be hard put
to find better value. / 11.15 pm; no credit cards; no booking.

Galicia W10   **£ 17**   A★
323 Portobello Rd   0181-969 3539   5-1A   159
This Spanish establishment is one of the most genuinely
foreign-feeling restaurants in London, due in no small part to
the extensive patronage of the local Portobello Hispanic
community. Fish dishes, such as baked hake (£9) are
particularly good. The Sunday lunch, three courses, including
an English-style roast, is, at £7.50, particularly good value.
House wine is £6.50. / 11.30 pm; closed Mon; no Switch.

Garbo's W1   **£ 16**   –
42 Crawford St   262 6582   2-1A   160
The particular attraction of this Scandinavian restaurant
(one of the few in London), west of Baker Street, is the
wonderful value £8.95, all-you-can-eat smörgasbord lunch. At
dinner time, with dishes like Swedish pea soup (£2.75), their
'famous' meatballs (£5.25) and pan-fried salmon (£8.25), you
can still keep within our price limit, though it's not quite such
good value. House wine is £7.95. Greta really did live here.
/ 11.30 pm; closed Sat L & Sun D; no Switch.

The Gate W6   **£ 14**   A★
51 Queen Caroline St   0181-748 6932   6-1A   161
Though situated just a stone's throw from Hammersmith's
busiest traffic junction, this vegetarian restaurant, hidden
away off a courtyard, offers a good deal of tranquillity. The
food's pretty good too – pumpkin gruyère torte (£3.90), spicy
Thai fruit curry (£6.50) – and attracts a steady following
despite the obscure location. Puddings, such as Queen's peach
frangipani tart (£3.20), come especially recommended.
House wine is £7. / 11 pm; closed Mon L, Sat L & Sun.

El Gaucho SW3   **£ 14**   A★
Chelsea Fmrs' Mkt, 125 Sydney St   376 8514   4-3C   162
Especially on a sunny summer's day (when there is very
pleasant outside seating), this unpretentious restaurant –
housed in a shed in fashionable Chelsea Farmers' Market –
offers some of London's best budget eating. Sit at the outside
tables, and enjoy competent, basic cooking of imported
Argentinean steaks (£9.90 for sirloin or rump), grilled chicken
(£5.90 for half) together with a salad or baked potato
(£1.80). It's a BYO place – there's a rather expensive
off-licence next door. / 11 pm; closed Mon; no credit cards.

Geale's W8   £ 12   ★★
                                     163
2 Farmer St   727 7969   5-2B
West London's most famous fish and chip shop justifiably
retains its reputation as one of the best value inexpensive
eating places anywhere around Notting Hill. Located a few
steps from the tube, it draws a complete cross-section of
Londoners and visitors. Price are keen – staples such as
haddock and chips cost around £6.50, and the house wine is
£5.75. It's certainly a place everyone should try at least once,
perhaps for the three course £7.50 lunch – say soup, fish of
the day with chips, and apple crumble. There can be a long
wait to be seated. / 11 pm; closed Mon & Sun; no Amex; no booking.

Geeta NW6   £ 10   ★
                                     164
59 Willesden Ln   624 1713   1-1B
Stylish it is not, but this no-frills North Kilburn Gujarati
restaurant attracts quite a following with the quality of its
South Indian cooking. Prices really are low, with meat curries
under £3 and vegetable curries even less. Kingfisher lager is
£1.30 a bottle. / 10.45 pm, Fri & Sat 11.45 pm; no Switch.

Gilbert's SW7   £18*   ★★
                                     165
2 Exhibition Rd   589 8947   4-2C
This cosy, cramped restaurant, right by South Kensington
tube, has a culinary reputation belying its small size. The two
course menu – perhaps goat's cheese and lentil salad
followed by fish stew provençale – is £16 at dinner, but only
£11.50 at lunch. Coffee and fudge is £2 and, with house wine
at £8.75, you can stay within our price limit at lunchtime only.
/ 10 pm; closed Sat & Sun; no switch.

Gopal's in the City EC2   £ 15   🄰★
                                     166
89 Gt Eastern St   729 4218   8-1D
Recently established on the northern fringe of the City, near
Liverpool Street, this offshoot of the well known Soho
establishment offers surroundings which are comfortable
enough for business lunching, but which still have the feeling
of a 'real' Indian restaurant. The menu is practically exactly
the same as at the original. / 10.15 pm; closed Sun.

Gopal's of Soho W1   £ 15   ★
                                     167
12 Bateman St   434 1621   3-2A
One of central London's leading Indians, providing reliable
cooking and a warm welcome. Curries are around the £6 to
£7 mark, and a large bottle of Cobra is £3.50. / 11.30 pm;
no smoking area.

Gordon's Wine Bar WC2 £10 Ⓐ
47 Villiers St   930 1408   3-4D   168
*There's nowhere else quite like this decayingly atmospheric
basement, a stone's throw from Embankment tube. The fare
is basic but inexpensive – for example salads, or a selection
of cold meats (£5.40) or a cheese plate (£3.50). With house
wine at £7 a bottle, this is a jolly place to start an evening in
the West End – or you might well decide to spend the whole
evening here. In summer, unusually for such a central place,
they have a good number of outside tables. (Owing to building
work, Gordon's will be closed for a significant period in mid-
1995.)* / 9 pm; closed Sat & Sun; no credit cards; no booking.

Gourmet Pizza Company £14 ★
Gabriels Whf, Upper Ground, SE1   928 3188   8-3A   169
Meranthun Way, SW19   0181-545 0310   6-2B   170
Canary Whf, E14   712 9192   1-3D   171
*For once the name says it all – these bright if slightly spartan
pizzerias really do offer consistently interesting, rather
unusual pizzas, perhaps bacon and goat's cheese, priced
from £4.95 to £7.95. Puddings, say baked lemon and sultana
cheesecake, are £2.95 and the house wine is £7.95. On a
warm summer evening, the Gabriel's Wharf branch, with its
riverside terrace, offers possibly the best panoramic view of
any restaurant in London.* / 10.30 pm - Midnight; no smoking area;
no booking.

Granary W1 £13 –
39 Albermarle St   493 2978   2-2B   172
*'Wholesome' is perhaps the word that best captures the spirit
of this long-established, waiter-assisted cafeteria, just off
Piccadilly. It offers hearty, fairly simple hot dishes (perhaps
casserole of lamb, £7.50), salads and tempting cakes. Prices
are all on the high side for a cafeteria – house wine at £8.50
does nothing to diminish this impression.* / 7.30 pm Mon-
Thurs, 8 pm F; closed Sat L & Sun; no credit cards.

Granita N1 £17* Ⓐ★★
127 Upper St   226 3222   7-2D   173
*This bare, rather noisy, modern restaurant is an Islington
favourite and has a widespread and justified reputation for its
Mediterranean cooking. At dinner time, prices are a touch
outside our range, but at lunch the £11.50 two course menu
(three courses for £13.50) offers good value. You might have
a salad of avocado, oak leaves, radiccio and pink grapefruit,
followed by rack of lamb and, if you go for pudding, chocolate
tart. Coffee is £1.25, and house wine £8.50.* / 10.30 pm; closed
Mon & Tue L; no Amex & no Switch.

45

Greek Valley NW8 £14 ★★

174

130 Boundary Rd   624 3217   7-3A

This friendly, family-run taverna just north of St John's Wood offers food as good as you will find in London at these sorts of prices. The à la carte menu is not expensive (most main dishes are about £6), and there are also a number of fixed price menus, for example three courses for £7.95 (Mon-Thu), and selections of meze at £8.50 and £10.95. House wine is £6.50 per bottle. For parties of 8 or more who order in advance there is a very good value, four course £10 meal. / Midnight; closed Sat L & Sun; no Amex & no Switch.

Grill St Quentin SW3 £14* ★

175

3 Yeoman's Rw   581 8377   4-2C

This large, well spaced Knightsbridge basement brasserie is under the same management as the more prominent Brasserie St Quentin in the Brompton Road. We find this place a touch on the antiseptic side, but it undoubtedly has its supporters, especially for those in search of calm in this hectic and expensive part of town. Like its sibling establishment, it offers a very good value £9 two course meal for lunch and for dinner before 7.30pm. See also the Savoy Group August offer. / 11.30 pm.

Häagen-Dazs £ 4 –

14 Leicester Sq, WC2   287 9577   3-3B 176
Unit 6, Covent Gdn, WC2   240 0436   3-3D 177
83 Gloucester Rd, SW7   373 9988   4-2B 178
88 Queensway, W2   229 0668   5-1C 179
75 Hampstead High St, NW3   794 0646   7-2A 180

Brilliant value they are not (you do have to pay for all that sexy advertising), but for a quick, luscious treat, these smart ice-cream parlours do offer a not-too-pricey fix of their popular ices. From the nineteen flavours, you can create your own sundae (£1.95 to £3.25 – toppings 45p cold, 65p hot). The Leicester Square branch is worth remembering for a post-cinema treat. / 11 pm, later weekends; no credit cards; no smoking; no booking.

Haandi NW1 £10 ★

181

161 Drummond St   383 4557   7-4C

The smartest of the restaurants in the 'Little India' near Euston Station is unusual for offering meat as well as vegetarian dishes. At lunchtime especially, it's worth making a detour for their £5.50 buffet. Even at dinner time, though, the place is not particularly expensive, with the barbecue mixed grill at £6.95 being the top price item. A bottle of Kingfisher is £1.50. Note that upstairs is much nicer than the basement. / 11.15 pm, Sat & Sun 11.45 pm; closed Sat L; no Switch.

Hamine W1   £ 8   ★
84 Brewer St   439 0785   2-2B   182
*This bustling, Soho Japanese canteen is a popular choice for a
budget snack. They serve a wide range of Japanese noodle
('ramen') dishes which are more or less a complete meal
(£7.50). Other popular dishes are their mincemeat
dumplings, and grilled pork (both £4) – miso soup is 50p. A
bottle of Sapporo costs £2.* / 2.30 am, Sat 1.30 am, Sun midnight;
no credit cards; no booking.

Harbour City W1   £ 14   ★★
46 Gerrard St   439 7859   3-3B   183
*At lunch, this large Chinatown establishment is one of the
better bets for dim sum. They have a good selection (for
£1.60 to £2.40) on an easy-to-understand menu which
includes a number of quite unusual dishes. Baked mini pork
pies, prawn or shark's fin dumplings, and crabmeat with
coriander are all popular choices. NB: our rating relates to
lunchtime only – in the evening, the cooking is pretty ordinary
by Chinatown standards. Most main dishes cost between
£4.90 and £6.90, and a can of Tsing Tao beer is £1.90.*
/ 11.15 pm, Fri & Sat 11.45 pm.

Hard Rock Café W1   £ 14   Ⓐ
150 Old Pk Ln   629 0382   2-3B   184
*The queue to get in to this famous Mayfair burger-joint is an
institution in itself (though you can cheat – if you book, you
can wait for a table in the bar instead). Once you're in, they
look after you very efficiently, and most people seem to enjoy
the experience of eating surrounded by rock memorabilia and
punishingly loud music. The food is nothing special – that
famous burger will set you back £6.75, or you could have a
pig sandwich or salad for about the same price. A bottle of
Bud' is £2.30.* / 12.30 am, Fri & Sat 1 am; no smoking area.

Hong Kong WC2   £ 15   ★
6 Lisle St   287 0324   3-3A   185
*By the standards of Chinatown, this large, quite smart
establishment offers a good all-round 'package'. At lunchtime,
you can have dim sum (£1.50 to £2 each). Most of the
standard main courses are between £4.50 and £8.50, and
a Tsing Tao beer £2.* / 11 pm.

Hope & Sir Loin EC1   £11*   –
94 Cowcross St   253 8525   8-1B   186
*Breakfast at one of the Smithfield pubs (licensed to serve ale
from dawn because of the local meat market) is something of
a London institution. The pleasant Sir Loin dining room
(above the Hope pub) caters for the committed carnivore
with its very, very meaty cooked breakfast (£7.50) –
though lighter options are available. You should book.*
/ L only; closed Sat & Sun.

Hoults SW17   **£17**   A
20 Bellevue Rd   0181-767 1858   6-2C   187
*It's the pretty location (on the edge of the common) and the
excellent atmosphere which are the reasons to visit this
buzzing Wandsworth brasserie. The food is quite basic
wine bar fare, for example grilled goat's cheese with roasted
peppers (£3.75), bangers and mash (£6.95) or home-made
fishcakes (£7.50). House wine is £7.50. / 10.45 pm.*

House on Rosslyn Hill NW3   **£16**   A
34a Rosslyn Hl   435 8037   7-2A   188
*This perennially buzzing Hampstead scene is a great budget
choice as a relaxed brunch, late-night, romantic or party
venue. But abandon any great expectations of the service or
the quality of the international dishes – for example burgers
(£4.95), mussels (£5.10) or wild mushroom tagliatelle (£6.45)
– as both can leave quite a lot to be desired. A bottle of
house wine is £8.50. / Midnight; no Amex.*

Hyde Park Hotel, Park Room SW1   **£15****   A
Knightsbridge   235 2000   2-3A   189
*If you want to inject a little grandeur into your day, you might
like to consider starting it off with a cooked breakfast (£15)
at this grand Knightsbridge hotel dining room, particularly
renowned for its views of Hyde Park. Needless to say, at other
times it's well out of our price range, except for the enjoyable
if not inexpensive afternoon tea.*

Ikkyu   **£15**   ★★
67 Tottenham Ct Rd, W1   636 9280   2-1C   190
7 Newport Pl, WC2   439 3554   3-3B   191
*The 'original' Ikkyu – the friendly basement near
Goodge Street – has long been known as one of the best
value Japanese spots in town. Now, there is a second, more
central, Chinatown branch offering similarly keenly priced
dishes in bare, but more stylish surroundings. Though details
differ slightly, both branches offer a range of inexpensive
options, such as grilled skewers at about £1 each and
have set meals – including inexpensive sushi options – for
under a tenner (the Tottenham Court Road branch is a little
more pricey in the evenings). Japanese beer in either branch
is £2.50. / 10.30 pm, WC2 Fri & Sat 11.30 pm; W1 closed Sat L & Sun;
W1 no Switch, WC2 no Amex; WC2 no smoking area.*

Imari WC1   **£15**   –
71 Red Lion St   405 0486   2-1D   192
*In the very thin area north of Holborn, this low-key Japanese
establishment is a popular lunch choice, especially amongst
local lawyers. The set lunch menus comprise a small
appetiser, soup, pickle, and fruit, together with a main dish,
which for £8.50 would be prawns or pork with rice, and for
£14 would be sushi and sashimi. A bottle of Sapporo is £2.80.
In the evening it is a little more expensive. / 10.30 pm; closed Sat
& Sun; no Switch.*

Inaho W2   **£ 16**   ★★
4 Hereford Rd   221 8495   5-1B   193
*A tiny gem of a Japanese café, located in the backwaters of
Bayswater. Service is friendly, if a little on the slow side, and
the quality of the cooking is some of the best in London at
the price. A popular choice to start would be aubergine with
miso paste (£4.50) and for a main dish, perhaps salmon
teriyaki or fried oysters (both about £8). A bottle of Kirin beer
is £2.30. / 11 pm; closed Sat L & Sun; no Amex & no Switch.*

India Club WC2   **£ 12**   –
143 Strand   836 0650   2-2D   194
*One of London's more unusual eateries is located on the first
floor of the Strand Continental Hotel (on the Aldwych) – a
very well worn dining room evoking images of Delhi.
The cooking is unpolished, but at the price no one's
complaining – the most expensive things on the menu are
tandoori chicken (four pieces, £8.60) and lamb pilau (£5.25).
BYO – there's no corkage – or pick up a pint from the
hotel bar. / 10 pm, Sun 8.30 pm; no credit cards; no booking.*

Italian Kitchen WC1   **£ 17**   ★
43 New Oxford St   836 1011   2-1C   195
*Near the British Museum, this unpretentious but comfortable
restaurant offers good north Italian cooking at reasonable
prices. You can always eat here within our price range from
the large selection of pizza, pasta and salads priced between
£6 and £7. Of special interest is the bargain menu of two
courses for £4.95, available from noon till 8pm – not a
culinary spectacular, but a good deal (you might have soup or
ham cake followed by pasta or chicken). Parents take note –
one child (under 12) per adult eats free. / 10.45 pm.*

The Jam SW3   **£ 14**   ★
289A King's Rd   352 8827   4-3C   196
*This '70s Chelsea bistro, with its unusual 'double decker',
boothed seating, has had new life breathed into it by the
team from Clapham's Buona Sera. The food is now much
improved, and includes a selection of pastas (around £5
to £6) and more substantial dishes (around £7 to £8).
House wine is £7.50. They are one of the best places in the
area open late, though the actual final time tends to vary
somewhat. / 2.30 am, Sat 3.30 am; closed Sun; no Amex & no Switch.*

Jigsaw W12   **£ 14**   Ⓐ
74 Askew Rd   0181-743 8002   1-3A   197
*In the thin area west of Shepherd's Bush, this jolly, budget
bistro is one of the better options (though not as good as
Adam's Café, opposite, which is run by the same people).
It's a very affordable place, the only option being the three
course set menu for £9.50. You get a fair selection – a typical
choice might be moules marinières, followed by lamb steak,
with apple tart to finish. House wine is £7.50. / 11 pm;
no credit cards.*

Jim Thompson's SW6   £17   Ⓐ
617 King's Rd   731 0999   4-4A   **198**
*It's not really the cooking which is the attraction of this lavishly
converted pub, but more the extremely buzzy atmosphere
which is good for a romantic encounter and already
generating a reputation as a good party venue.*
*The cooking mixes a variety of oriental influences. A la carte,
main dishes are about £5.50, but they offer a number of set
menus. For £12.95, the 'Grand Palace' offers two courses and
coffee. A bottle of house wine is £7.95. / 11 pm.*

Jimmy Beez W10   £17   ★
303 Portobello Rd   0181-964 9100   5-1A   **199**
*A favourite with Portobello trendies – especially during
summer, when the outside tables provide a favoured spot for
recovering from a hangover, while watching the world go by.
The menu of international light dishes is not especially cheap,
but it is well done. It is always possible to find dishes such as
home-made soup (£2.75), salmon and crab fishcakes (£6.75)
and tagliatelle (£5.50) on the menu, and, in the evening,
more expensive items too. House wine is £8. / 11 pm; no Switch.*

Jimmy's W1   £10   –
23 Frith St   437 9521   3-2A   **200**
*This tucked away Soho basement has been a budget
West End stand-by since 1948. It's the elderly staff who really
make the place and, though they're swift, you do not feel that
they are rushing you. The grub is cheap, hearty and not too
bad – taramasalata (£1.50), moussaka and chips (£4.50),
Greek pastries (£1.20). The house wine is similarly
inexpensive at £6.10 per bottle. / 11 pm, Thu Fri & Sat 11.30 pm;
closed Sun; no credit cards.*

Jin Kichi NW3   £13   –
73 Heath St   794 6158   7-1A   **201**
*Basic but pleasant Hampstead Japanese café with a wide-
ranging, reasonably priced menu. The good quality yakitori
(grilled Japanese skewers) are typically £1 each and there is
also a limited choice of other dishes. Sake is £5 for a large
pot, and a Japanese beer is £2.20. / 11.30 pm; Mon, Wed, Thu & Fri
D only, open L & D Sun.*

Joe's Brasserie SW6   £16   Ⓐ
130 Wandsworth Br Rd   731 7835   6-1B   **202**
*Loud, permanently packed Fulham brasserie which is a
popular hang-out for a raucous, youngish crowd. There's
absolutely nothing notable about the quality of the cooking,
but this is quite a fun place and worth bearing in mind for a
budget bash. They offer two course set meals – at lunch for
£6.90 (including a glass of wine) and at dinner for £9.90. In
the evening, starters are £3 to £5 and burgers, for example,
are around £7. House wine is £7.50. / 10.45 pm; no smoking area.*

Joe's Wine Bar SW11   £14   𝔸 ★
33 Lavender Hl   228 2960   6-2C   203
This atmospheric Battersea wine bar offers a consistent
package, and is one of the best bets in the area. Burgers and
fishcakes (both £6.50) are typical of the menu of staples,
cooked with care, and there are also some more expensive
dishes – for example, a starter of pan-fried tiger prawns at
£4.50, and char-grilled duck's breast at £8.95. House wine
is £7.75. / 11.30 pm; closed Mon; no Amex.

Kalamaras, Mega W2   £15   𝔸 ★★
76-78 Inverness Mews   727 9122   5-2C   204
The grander sibling of Kalamaras, Micro (see next), offering
greater comfort and atmosphere, at only slightly higher prices
– no BYO, though. / Midnight; D only, closed Sun.

Kalamaras, Micro W2   £11   𝔸 ★★
66 Inverness Mews   727 5082   5-2C   205
Though it's over twenty years old, this cosy, cramped and tatty
taverna (in a difficult-to-find mews) shows little sign of running
out of steam, and the dishes are, with the odd exception, top
notch. You might choose from items such as melitzanosalata
(aubergine dip, £2.60) and dolmades (£4.85), or, for a
big meal, go for their £12.50 set menu. The place is
unlicensed, so you must BYO – beer is not allowed. / 11 pm;
D only; closed Sun; no Switch.

Karahi NW6   £12   ★
212 West End Ln   431 3074   1-1B   206
This once elegant, now slightly worn basement Indian is worth
considering if you should find yourself in the West Hampstead
area. The service is friendly and the cooking, which has
East African influences, is unusually light for its type.
Vegetarian main dishes are about £3, meat curries about
£5.50 and the house speciality is Talapia fish (£5.95).
Kenyan Tusker beer is £2 a bottle. / 11 pm; D only.

Kastoori SW17   £10   ★★
188 Upper Tooting Rd   0181-767 7027   6-2C   207
The mother of an acquaintance of ours turned down a
farewell-to-London dinner at the Ritz, asking instead to pay a
return visit to this humble Indian vegetarian restaurant in
deepest Tooting – as you may gather, it offers some of
London's best and best value ethnic cooking. Nothing costs
much over £4, with specialities such as green banana curry
(£3.75), or corn curry (£3.25), and the menu includes a wide
selection of breads, poori and other starters. You can drink
passion fruit juice (£1.50), or a pint of Kingfisher is £1.80.
/ 10.30 pm; closed Mon & Tue L; no Amex & no Switch.

Kensington Place W8 £19* A★★
201-205 Kensington Ch St   727 3184   5-2B   208
This large, fashionable, very noisy goldfish bowl of a place –
for many people the 'benchmark' modern British restaurant –
remains enormously successful and popular. Dinner here is
not really feasible within our price range, but the three course
set lunch for £13.50 – perhaps soupe au pistou, grilled tuna
with aubergine, and raspberry jelly – offers excellent value.
House wine is £8.75. / 11.45 pm; no Amex.

Kettners W1 £14 A
29 Romilly St   437 6437   3-2A   209
This was once a very famous establishment, popular with the
Edwardian aristocracy, and much period charm remains at
what is probably London's grandest budget restaurant – now
a PizzaExpress. It used to be one of our top budget tips –
especially for a celebration – but, of late, standards seem to
have become rather variable. Still, it's worth a try, for a pizza
or a burger (both about £6) or a salad (£5 to £8). There are
large champagne and wine bars where you can wait for a
table. House wine is £7.95. / Midnight; no booking.

Khan's W2 £11 A
13-15 Westbourne Gr   727 5420   5-1C   210
This chaotic, cavernous Bayswater Indian is as notorious for
its aggressive, rushed service as it is famous for its low, low
prices. If you go forewarned and don't expect to linger, then it
can be great fun, especially for a budget group meal. Main
dishes are between £2.50 and £4.25, and a bottle of Cobra
is £2.25. / 11.45 pm; no Switch.

Khan's of Kensington SW7 £15 A
3 Harrington Rd   581 2900   4-2B   211
Especially, perhaps, for those for whom Indian food is a
novelty, this conveniently located spot (right by South
Kensington tube) has a lot going for it. The food is not
startling, but it's quite reliable, and the level of comfort is well
above average. You can always eat here within our budget,
and they also offer a two course lunch with coffee for £7.50
(say a kebab, lamb or chicken curry, with rice), and a Sunday
buffet for £6.95. A pint of Kingfisher is £2.50. / 11.30 pm.

Khyber Pass SW7 £13 ★
21 Bute St   589 7311   4-2B   212
Remarkable to look at it most certainly is not, but this well
established Indian restaurant near South Kensington tube is
quite well known, thanks to its convenient location and its
modest prices. Curries are around £4 to £5 and a bottle of
Kingfisher will set you back £1.60. / 11.30 pm; no Switch.

King's Road Café SW3   £ 11   A★

206 King's Rd   351 1211   4-3C   ²¹³

As the King's Road in Chelsea is infamously thinly provided
with decent eating places, this café, hidden away on the first
floor of the Habitat shop, is especially worth knowing about.
It's a good place to start the day off (from 10am) with a
croissant (75p), or for a shopping lunch-stop. You might have
a Mediterranean salad, or a plate of home-made pasta
(both around a fiver). In the afternoon, they do a good value
cream tea (£2.90). House wine is £8. / open shop hours, L till 3 pm;
no credit cards; no smoking area.

Krungtap SW10   £ 10   ★

227 Old Brompton Rd   259 2314   4-2A   [214]

Located by the cross-roads with the Earl's Court Road, this
highly popular, extremely cramped Thai restaurant is the
epitome of a candle-lit, cheap and cheerful local spot (and
also useful for a super-budget celebration). Everyone tries
very hard and, especially given the unusually low prices for the
area, the odd slip in the cooking is easily forgiven. Set menus
(for two people) start at £8 a head, and you can eat à la
carte for about the same price. Singha beer is £2.
/ 10.30 pm; D only; no Amex.

Lahore Kebab House E1   £ 8   ★★

2 Umberston St   488 2551   1-2D   [215]

Few are disappointed by the pilgrimage to this ultra-basic
Indian canteen in Whitechapel, where the grotty décor and
worn Formica tables only add to the experience. The point of
the trip is the range of excellent kebab dishes — some of the
best value budget food in London. It would be tough to spend
over a tenner here, and you must BYO. / Midnight; no credit cards.

Lalbag W11   £ 11   ★

188 Westbourne Gr   727 7558   5-1B   [216]

This Notting Hill Indian has a strong local reputation for
offering all-round value. Compared to the usual standards,
it's a comfortable place and its Bangladeshi dishes are
carefully cooked. Tandoori chicken is £3.85, around the
same price as most of the other main course dishes.
/ Midnight; no Switch.

Lansdowne NW1   £ 15   A★

90 Gloucester Ave   483 0409   7-2B   [217]

Trendy, buzzing Primrose Hill pub/restaurant which offers
relatively ambitious modern British cooking — it's a very
popular place, and often very crowded. You choose from the
blackboard at the bar — perhaps coriander soup (£3.50)
followed by salt cod brandade (£6) — and your choice is then
brought to your table. House wine is £8. / 10 pm; closed Mon L;
no credit cards; book Sun L only.

Latymers W6   £ 9   ★
157 Hammersmith Rd   0181-741 2507   1-3B   *218*
From the outside, this is not the best looking of pubs.
The inside isn't so different, but the Thai food on offer in
the annex is good quality and the best cooking available in
this very thin area. Most main courses are £4 or so, and on
weekday lunches they offer one plate dishes including rice for
£3.25. A bottle of Singha is £2.20. / 10 pm; D only; closed Sun;
no Switch.

Launceston Place W8   £19*   A★★
1a Launceston Pl   937 6912   4-1B   *219*
Located in an extremely pretty road in Kensington, this
romantic English townhouse restaurant offers two options for
those on a budget. At lunch, there's a two course menu for
£13.50. More unusually, after 10pm, they have a modestly-
priced supper menu, from which you might choose baked
aubergine at £4.50, or spinach and fresh herb risotto (£4 as
a starter, £7.50 as a main course). House wine
is £8.50. / 11.30 pm; closed Sat L & Sun D.

Laurent NW2   £ 15   ★★
428 Finchley Rd   794 3603   1-1B   *220*
Devotees of couscous should seek out this northerly café in
the area west of Hampstead Heath. Five types are offered –
from the vegetarian (£6.60) to the Royale (£10.25) – and
there are no other main course options. Start with brik à
l'oeuf (£2.60), or finish with crêpes suzettes (£3.20).
House wine is £8. / 11 pm; closed Sun; no Switch.

Leadenhall Tapas Bar EC3   £ 13   A
27 Leadenhall Mkt   623 1818   8-3D   *221*
With its very picturesque location, looking down on the
Victorian elegance of Leadenhall Market, this civilised bar has,
for the City, an unusually attractive atmosphere. A bargain the
place is not, and house wine is £8.95 a bottle. Still, at lunch
most dishes are under £6, and the place is worth
remembering for a snack with style in a pricey area.
/ L only; closed Sat & Sun; no booking.

Lemonia NW1   £ 15   A★
89 Regent's Pk Rd   586 7454   7-3B   *222*
Something of a phenomenon (so book ahead), this large,
bustling, Primrose Hill Greek is more brasserie than taverna
and attracts a diverse, fashionable crowd. A fun place, but the
food is not the least of the attractions. Many choose the good
value £10.50 selection of meze. House wine is £9.25
a bottle. / 11.30 pm; closed Sat L & Sun D; no Amex & no Switch.

The Lexington W1 £14 ★
223

Lexington St   434 3401   2-2C

This slightly louche spot, hidden away in Soho, is at its best when the piano is playing. There are few central places which save their best value offer for the evening, but here it's the £10 set dinner menu which is the particular attraction. For this, you get two courses, perhaps grilled merguez sausage with couscous and garlic, followed by sun-dried tomato risotto and coffee. House wine is £9. / 11 pm; closed Sat L & Sun; no Switch.

Lindsay House W1 £15* A ★
224

21 Romilly St   439 0450   3-3A

Dinner is far out of our price range at this richly furnished, romantic, olde worlde Soho townhouse. However, the weekday lunchtime menu of two courses (including coffee) for £10 (or three courses for £14.75) allows those on a budget to enjoy these sumptuous and calming surroundings, together with a modest degree of culinary excitement. A typical lunch might be rabbit and leek terrine with mustard dressing, followed by breast of guinea fowl with aubergine fricassee. House wine is £9.50. / Midnight; no Switch.

Lisboa Patisserie W10 £ 3 A ★★
225

57 Golborne Rd   0181-968 5242   5-1A

At weekends, you will be lucky to get a seat at this Portobello pâtisserie, which is shared between the local Portuguese community and hordes of black-clad trendies. It is one of London's top cheap eats – many of the pastries are absolutely delicious and everything is ridiculously inexpensive. Cakes are priced from 35p and a custard tart (pasteis de natas – the house speciality) is 50p. Savoury rolls and croissants are 70p to £1.35, and a cup of coffee is 55p. / 8 pm; no credit cards.

Lobster Pot SE11 £20* A ★
226

3 Kennington Ln   582 5556   1-3C

It's been something of a miracle to establish a quality restaurant in the unpropitious area south of the Elephant and Castle, but this mega-kitsch fish parlour (done out as a sunken galleon) is establishing a solid reputation. It's out of our price range in the evening, but there is a £14.50 set lunch, and house wine at £9.50. / 11 pm; closed Mon & Sun.

Los Remos W2 £13 ★
227

38a Southwick St   723 5056   5-1D

The cosy basement tapas bar at this Paddington establishment, offers good cheer in an area short on welcoming places (and a better bet than the rather uninspired upstairs restaurant). Prices for tapas start at £1.50 for a Spanish omelette, with langoustine and prawn dishes being the most expensive, at £6.50. On Thursdays, Fridays and Saturdays, there is live guitar music and the place is licensed to 1 am. The wine list here has one of the best Spanish selections in London – the house's choice is £7.50 a bottle. / Midnight; closed Sun; no Switch.

Mandeer W1   **£12**   A★
                                                        237
21 Hanway Pl   323 0660   3-1A

Stuck in the unpromising area north of Tottenham Court Road tube, this vegetarian Indian has been a 'find' for over twenty years now, and offers an atmospheric refuge from Oxford Street. At lunchtime they open the 'refectory' – a cafeteria where few dishes cost more than a fiver. Prices in the 'Aladdin's Cave' of a restaurant, open for lunch and dinner, are only a little higher. Wash your meal down with a bottle of Kingfisher for £1.30. / 10 pm; closed Sun; no smoking.

Manzara W11   **£12**   ★
                                                        238
24 Pembridge Rd   727 3062   5-2B

This excellent Turkish café, to the rear of a take-away, is one of the best deals around Notting Hill Gate and, for a simple but agreeable meal at bargain basement prices, is hard to beat. Meze at just £3.95 for six dishes offers good value, especially to the hungry. Other dishes, such as kebabs, are if anything better, and nothing costs over a fiver. Good pastries are a further attraction. House wine is £7.45. / 11.30 pm; no smoking area.

Marché Mövenpick W1   **£11**   ★
                                                        239
Swiss Centre, Leicester Sq   734 1291   3-4A

This large self-service food market, below Leicester Square's Swiss Centre, is worth bearing in mind for a superior snack right in the centre of town – it's especially convenient for the movies or theatre. There is a wide selection of relatively inexpensive choices (soup of the day is £1.50 or less), and you can watch fresh, tasty dishes such as chicken breast (£4) or salmon steak (£5.30) being cooked up according to your order. Beware that drinks prices – a glass of wine is £2.45 – are no bargain. / Midnight; no smoking area.

Marine Ices NW3   **£12**   A★
                                                        240
8 Haverstock Hl   485 3132   7-2B

Opposite Chalk Farm tube, this family-run Italian has, since the '20s, dished up some of London's best ice-cream and sorbets. It is more than just a treat for the kids however, and even in the evenings you must book to enjoy its friendly, bustling charm. They do OK pizzas and pasta for around a fiver. It is the ices (a couple of pounds and up) which are the real point of a visit here, however, and, on Sunday, they are all that are available. / 11 pm; no Amex; no smoking area.

Maroush   **£11**   A★
                                                        241
1) 21 Edgware Rd, W2   724 5024   5-1D
2) 38 Beauchamp Pl, SW3   581 5434   4-1C   242

These smart restaurants – part of London's best known Lebanese chain – have café/take-aways popular with the Arab community. The attraction is the combination of reasonable prices – £2.75 for kebabs, falafel sandwiches and the like – and the fact that they keep seriously late hours. / W2. 1.30 am; SW3, 4 am; no Switch & no cheques.

Mars WC2 £16 A★
243

59 Endell St   240 8077   3-1C

You've probably got to be the right age-group, and in the right state of mind to enjoy this contrived but buzzy restaurant on the trendy northern fringe of Covent Garden. The dishes – mainstream examples being goat's cheese with spinach in puff pastry (£3.50) or Cajun salmon (£8.50) – sometimes tend to the over-experimental, but they generally offer pretty good value. House wine is £7.95. / Midnight; closed Sat L & Sun; no credit cards.

Mas Café W11 £19* A★
244

6-8 All Saints Rd   243 0969   5-1B

The fact that this street used to be notorious for drugs dealing still adds a slight 'frisson' to a visit to this hip Mediterranean bar/brasserie, which is particularly popular with the Notting Hill in-crowd. The food is reliable and interesting – typical dishes might be duck liver salad with chorizo (£3.50) and free-range chicken with lemon and green olives (£7.90). Vegetables are a couple of pounds extra. At weekends, there's an all-day breakfast (£5.95). House wine is £9. / Midnight; Winter, Mon-Fri closed L; no Amex; no smoking area.

Mayflower W1 £16 ★★
245

68-70 Shaftesbury Ave   734 9207   3-3A

Externally, this Chinese restaurant may be pretty undistinguished, but it is arguably the culinary star of Chinatown. (It also offers what is almost certainly the best food in London available in the early hours of the morning.) There are, of course, set menus (from £11.50), but if you want to scale the heights, you are much better advised to go for the more adventurous dishes à la carte. Tsing Tao beer is £1.80 a bottle. / 4 am; D only; no Switch.

Mekong SW1 £16 A
246

46 Churton St   834 6896   2-4B

This Vietnamese/Chinese restaurant in Pimlico has long had a reputation as a reasonably convivial place in rather a thin area. There are set menus at £12 to £15, or you can go à la carte for about the same amount. Tiger beer is £2 for half a pint. / 11.30 pm; no Amex & no Switch.

Melati W1 £15 ★
247

21 Great Windmill St   437 2745   2-2C

This tightly packed, quite cosy Malaysian bistro offers a good value overall package. It's one of the best places off Piccadilly Circus and is ideal for a quick and filling meal pre- or post-theatre. There is a long menu, from which most of the dishes (which are in the £5 to £6 price range) are well-prepared and tasty. A can of Tiger is £2.25. / 11.30 pm, Fri & Sat 12.30 am; no Switch.

Le Mercury N1   £12   A
140A Upper St   354 4088   7-3D   248
*A convenient location in the centre of Islington, late hours
and reasonable prices are the strengths of this bohemian
establishment. The food is formulaic bistro fare, but that
seems to do little to dent the place's popularity. For dinner,
all starters (for example, goat's cheese salad) are £2.25,
all main dishes (such as medallions of pork) are £5.45,
and puddings (perhaps pancake with vanilla ice cream
and chocolate walnut sauce) are £1.95. During the
daytime (until 6pm), these prices are only £1, £3.50 and
50p respectively. House wine is £6.75.*
/ 1 am; no Amex & no Switch.

Meson Don Felipe SE1   £12   A★
53 The Cut   928 3237   8-4A   249
*A flamenco guitarist (most nights) helps to create an
atmosphere which seems surprisingly like rural Spain for
somewhere not far from the Old Vic. The tapas (from mixed
salad at £1.75 to Mediterranean prawns at £4.50) are very
good, and the place is often packed. House wine is £7.95.*
/ 11 pm; no Amex; book pre 1 pm only.

Meson Doña Ana W11   £12   A★
37 Kensington Pk Rd   243 0666   5-1A   250
*Though it lacks a guitarist, this buzzy, younger-scene bar
in the trendy heart of Notting Hill offers essentially the
same good value package as its southerly brother,
Meson Don Felipe. / 11.30 pm; no Amex.*

Mildreds W1   £10   ★
58 Greek St   494 1634   3-2A   251
*This basic Soho café is one of the few central places which
offers an interesting, evolving menu of vegetarian fare.
It's also unusual in being open in the evening, so it offers
inexpensive pre-theatre snacking possibilities. Sample dishes
might be falafel or stir-fried vegetables (both £3.90), followed
perhaps by fresh fruit salad or baked rum and chocolate
pudding (both £2.50). House wine is £6.95. / 11 pm;
closed Sun; no credit cards; no smoking; need 6+ to book.*

Ming W1   £17   A★
35-36 Greek St   734 2721   3-2A   252
*If the Chinatown maelstrom is not entirely to your taste,
venture just over the border into this Soho establishment,
where the food is, if anything, better and the level of
civilisation much higher. In the evening, you can comfortably
explore the menu of dishes from all over China, within our
price range. House wine is £8.25. From noon to 7pm
(so, useful pre-theatre), there's a three course menu with tea
or coffee for £10, or you could have a 'Ming bowl' for £6
or less. / 11.45 pm; closed Sun; no Switch; no smoking area.*

Mon Petit Plaisir W8 £19[*] 🅐★
33C Holland St 937 3224 4–1A [253]
*This pretty, romantic and tightly packed Kensington bistro
offers quality, traditional French cooking. The lunch menu
(there is no early evening option) is essentially the same as at
Mon Plaisir (below), but here the three course menu does not
include wine, coffee or service.* / 10.30 pm; closed Sat L & Sun.

Mon Plaisir WC2 £14[*] 🅐★★
21 Monmouth St 836 7243 3–2B [254]
*According to an American couple encountered on a recent
visit to this quintessential Theatreland bistro, the place is just
as good now as it was on their first visit in 1957. It still makes
an extremely congenial place to kick off an evening, and with
their £13.95 pre-theatre offer (served from 6pm, and you
must be out by 8pm), you get really great value. The menu
includes not only three courses – you might have soup, a
fricassee of meats in puff pastry with a bavaroise of red fruit
to finish – but also a glass of wine, a cup of coffee and
service. The set lunch menu is the same price, but, as it
excludes wine, coffee and service, it is only just within our
price limit. House wine is £8.50.* / 11.15 pm; closed Sat L & Sun.

Mongolian Barbecue £14 –
31 Parson's Gn Ln, SW6 371 0433 6–1B [255]
61 Gloucester Rd, SW7 581 8747 4–2B [256]
187 South Ealing Rd, W5 0181-569 7171 1–3A [257]
38 Haven Gn, W5 0181-998 2066 1–3A [258]
183 Lavender Hl, SW11 228 2660 6–2C [259]
147 Upper R'mnd Rd, SW15 0181-780 9252 6–2B [260]
162 The Broadway, SW19 0181-545 0021 6–2B [261]
*Weird as it may seem to suggest a place where your meal
may end up almost completely inedible, many people –
especially groups – love these oriental-inspired restaurants
where you make up your own recipes. Delight when someone
else's combination of meats, oils and spices goes horribly
wrong is all part of the fun. It's not expensive – £9.95 for
as much as you can bear to eat. Note that groups over seven
must have a £10.95 menu which includes a starter. House
wine is £6.95.* / 11pm; D only.

Moshi Moshi Sushi EC2 £ 7 ★★
Unit 24, Liverpool St Station 247 3227 8–2D [262]
*For an original and economical snack – a rare commodity in
the City – this Japanese café overlooking the platforms at
Liverpool Street station is the place. Plates of top-quality sushi
snake around a conveyor belt atop the bar. Grab what you
want and then pay according to the number and colour of the
plates taken – they are priced from 90p to £1.80.*
/ 9pm; closed Sat & Sun; no Amex; no smoking; no booking.

Mr Kong WC2   £ 12   ★★

21 Lisle St   437 7341   3-3A   263

*Few Chinatown restaurants could be accused of being good
all-rounders – this is one of the exceptions. The staff are
agreeable and the setting – at least if you stay upstairs –
may be cramped but at least it's cheerful by the local
standards. The food is well above average. Main dishes are
priced from £5.20 and there is also a large selection of quite
unusual specials mostly priced from £7.50 to £11. Tsing Tao
beer is £1.80 a bottle.* / 1.45 am; no Switch.

Museum St Café WC1   £18*   ★★

47 Museum St   405 3211   2-1C   264

*This successful (and quite recently expanded) foodie café, just
down the road from the British Museum, has made its name
by offering good quality, simple modern British cooking. At
night, they're out of our price range, but the two course lunch
menu at £12 offers the opportunity to try the place out.
You might have, say, yellow split pea soup with spiced
yoghurt, followed by guinea fowl pie. House wine is £8.25.*
/ 9.30 pm; closed Sat & Sun; no smoking.

Mustards Bistro à Vin EC1   £ 17   Ⓐ

62-63 Long Ln   600 1111   8-1B   265

*If you are looking for a real dinner at a reasonable price, it's
well worth considering a trip to this Smithfield spot, which is
atmospherically located right opposite the recently refurbished
market building. Three courses from the set menu come for
only £10 (or two for £7.50) – you might choose smoked
herring with new potatoes, Toulouse sausages with lentils and
an iced chocolate mousse. At lunchtime, it's a bit more pricey,
but a main-course sized helping from 'le Chariot' of hors
d'oeuvres (£7.95) offers good value. House wine is £7.95.*
/ 11 pm; closed Sat & Sun; no Switch.

Mustoe Bistro NW1   £ 12   ★

73 Regent's Pk Rd   586 0901   7-3B   266

*If Central Castings were required to supply a budget bistro, it
would look something like this tiny, unpretentious place in
Primrose Hill. Standards are high, though, for starters such as
egg Madras (£1.50) or veal pâté (£2.50) and main courses
such as vegetable saté (£5.50) and venison casserole (£6.20).
House wine is £6.50.* / 11.15 pm; D only Mon-Sat, open L & D Sun;
no Amex & no Switch.

Naked Turtle SW14   £ 17   Ⓐ★

505 Upper Richmond Rd   0181-878 1995   6-2A   267

*It may be rather remotely situated, in East Sheen, but this
jolly wine bar has quite a reputation as a place for a good
night out. The loud jazz, played nightly, is arguably the
greatest attraction, but, of late, exotic dishes have also
become quite a feature, with smoked ostrich salad (£4.25),
medallions of kangaroo (£9.95), and char-grilled crocodile tail
(£8.95) joining more usual wine bar staples on the menu.
They do a three course business lunch during the week for
£7.95. House wine is £8.95.* / 11 pm; no smoking area.

Namaste E1   £15   ★★

30 Alie St   488 9242   1-2D   268

Indian cooking as good as you will find anywhere in London is beginning to make quite a name for this unpretentious restaurant, rather obscurely located around the corner from Tower Hill. It has one of the most interesting menus of its type, ranging across all of India and including tandoori, Goan, South Indian and Parsi dishes, together with regularly changing specialities. Examples are mussels in hot pickled masala (£3.95), fish rolled in green coconut chutney (£7.35) and pheasant stuffed with chicken (£7.50). Kingfisher beer is £1.70 a bottle. / 11 pm; closed Sat L & Sun.

Nautilus NW6   £12   ★

27 Fortune Gn Rd   435 2532   1-1B   269

It's primarily the quality of the fish (fried in matzo meal) which is the draw to this rather kitsch, kosher chippie in West Hampstead. Nearly all the fish are priced between £7 and £10, or chicken and chips is a fiver. Soup to start is £1 or ice-cream to finish £1.80. House wine is £7 (or £5 if you can drink retsina). / 10.15 pm; closed Sun; no credit cards; no booking.

Nayab SW6   £16   ★

309 New King's Rd   731 6993   6-1B   270

The quality of the cooking at this Parson's Green Indian restaurant is very much above average, and, by the standards of subcontinental places, the décor is of quite a high standard (if perhaps a touch oppressive). Curries are about £6, and Kingfisher £2.15 a bottle. Lunchtime opening is a recent innovation. / Midnight; no smoking area.

Neal's Yard Dining Rooms WC2   £9   ★

14 Neal's Yd   379 0298   3-2C   271

If you're looking for a tasty, inexpensive, meal near Covent Garden, you could do very much worse than this vegetarian 'World Café' – especially in summer, when the large windows open onto the yard below. The menu consists of street food from around the globe, and generally comprises four light meals at £3.85 (such as Mexican tortillas) and five more substantial main meals for £5.85 (perhaps an Indian thali, or West African groundnut stew). It's a no-smoking place, and you may well have to share a table. Drink fruit juice or lassi (£1.60), or BYO (no corkage). / Winter, 5 pm ex Wed & Fri 7.30 pm; summer, 7.30 pm, Sat & Sun 5 pm; closed Sat & Sun; no credit cards; no smoking; no booking.

New World W1   £13   –

Gerrard Pl   734 0677   3-3A   272

One of the sights of Chinatown, this huge, gaudy 600-seat restaurant is best experienced for lunchtime dim sum – you choose your dishes (very reasonably priced at about £1.50 to £2.80 each) from the various trolleys which career around the vast dining rooms. Dinner is perfectly acceptable, but more ordinary. House wine is £6.75. / 11.45 pm; no Switch.

Nizam SW5 £17 🄰
152 Old Brompton Rd   373 0024   4-2B 273
This South Kensington Indian has prices which are quite
reasonable for the area, and benefits from a comfortable,
well spaced and quite attractive setting. Curries are
generally around £6, and Kingfisher lager is £2.20.
The Sunday buffet lunch is £7.95. / 11.45 pm; no Switch.

Nontas NW1 £12 ★
14 Camden High St   387 4579   7-3C 274
This classic Camden Town taverna is one of the more reliable
Greek places in town, and in summer boasts the particular
attraction of a fair-sized garden. Prices are low – moussaka,
say, is £5.30. Another option is the selection of meze (£8.75).
House wine is £8.60 per litre. There is also an ouzerie
(café/wine bar) which is open all day from breakfast
(when they serve Greek pastries) – most of the good range
of small dishes there cost less than £2. / 11.30 pm; closed Sun;
no Switch.

C Notarianni & Sons SW11 £15 ★
142 Battersea High St   228 7133   6-1C 275
The calzone is the star attraction at this Battersea pizza and
ice-cream parlour which has been in the same family for
generations. The place has quite an interesting art deco
interior, with jukebox, but the chairs seem designed to
discourage lingering. The hot dishes are generally around a
fiver, and house wine is £7.75. / 11.30 pm; closed Sat L & Sun;
no Amex & no Switch.

Noto £11 ★
2/3 Bassishaw Highwalk, EC2   256 9433   8-2C 276
7 Bread St, EC4   329 8056   8-2B 277
These no-frills, City Japanese noodle bars are most popular as
cheap lunchtime places, and good quality, very filling 'ramen'
dishes (£6 to £8) are served in both locations. Bread Street,
the smaller of the two, is a 'stop – eat – go' kind of place.
The larger, Barbican branch also serves a number of curries –
these are particularly popular as part of the lunchtime set
menus (£5.80 to £6.80), which also include rice and soup.
A bottle of Kirin beer is £1.80. / EC2 10 pm, Sat 9 pm – EC4 9 pm;
EC2 closed Sun, – EC4 closed Sat & Sun; EC2 no Amex and no credit cards at
lunch – EC4 no credit cards; EC2 no smoking at L; no booking.

O'Keefe's W1 £16 ★
19 Dering St   495 0878   2-2B 278
Trendy, self-consciously mimimalistic Mayfair corner
café/restaurant, offering fairly reliable cooking. As a starter
you might opt for vegetable soup (£2.75) or mixed pepper
quiche (£3.75), and as a main course Thai chicken salad or
lamb's liver Lyonnaise (both £7.50). At lunchtime, there are
also sandwiches (£3 to £4), some of them rather exotic.
House wine is £7.75. / 10 pm; Mon, Fri & Sat L only, closed Sun.

Odette's NW1 £17* A★★
130 Regent's Pk Rd   586 5486   7-3B   279

*Even at the grandest restaurant in north London – and a
romantic, multi-mirrored place it is, on Primrose Hill –
you can enjoy a three course set lunch (Mon-Fri) for £10.
You might have cream of Jerusalem artichoke and rocket
soup, followed by char-grilled plaice, and baked mascarpone
tart. House wine is £10.50.* / 10.30 pm; closed Sun D; no Switch.

Odette's Wine Bar NW1 £16 ★
130 Regent's Pk Rd   722 5388   7-3B   280

*The cellar of one of north London's most charming
restaurants provides a home for a high quality wine bar,
whose prices are much less elevated than those above.
You might start with soup (£2.50) and follow up with suckling
pigs' livers (£5.50) or baked cod with warm potato salad (£7).
House wine is £7.95. Sunday lunchtime – when you can enjoy
the wine-bar menu in the very smart upstairs restaurant – is
the best time to go.* / 10.30 pm; closed Sun D; no Switch.

Ognisko Polskie SW7 £14 A
55 Princess Gt, Exhibition Rd   589 4635   4-1C   281

*This time-warped South Kensington club for Polish expatriates
offers quite a good choice of dishes from its native cuisine.
If you go à la carte – herring (£3.80), borscht (£4), dumplings
(£7.80) – it's not especially inexpensive, but the budget
option, always available, is the £7.50 set menu, which
includes soup, a choice of two main courses and a pudding.
House wine is £8.40. (This is also a good place for tea and
cakes after a visit to the local museums.)* / 11 pm; no Switch.

Ye Olde Cheshire Cheese EC4 £14 A
145 Fleet St   353 6170   8-2A   282

*In winter, when the real coal fire is burning, this historic pub
on the fringe of the City offers one of the most authentic
tastes of olde England you will find in the metropolis.
Naturally, it's a bit touristy, but the fare is not really too bad.
In the restaurant, perhaps unsurprisingly, the top items are
steak and kidney pudding (£7.50) and roast beef (£7.95), or,
if you prefer something lighter, you could have a salad for
around £6.50. In the restaurant, Sam Smith's bitter is £1.78
a pint.* / 9 pm bar; 9.30 pm restaurant; only bar food Sun, closed Sun D.

Orangery W8 £11 A
Kensington Palace   376 0239   5-2C   283

*If you're looking for a light bite in a lovely setting, stroll
(in the summer only, of course) through the gardens to the
fine Queen Anne summer house of Kensington Palace.
Tea (£1.40), cakes (around £3) and scones (£3.15) are the
main attractions, but they also do soup (£2.80) and a range
of (fairly pricey) salads and light dishes. House wine is £9.95.*
/ 6 pm; no Amex & no Switch; no smoking.

Oriel SW1 £17 Ⓐ
50-51 Sloane Sq   730 2804   4-2D 284
You wouldn't expect the main strength of a prominently sited brasserie at the centre of fashionable London to be the food. You would be right, but the cooking – fairly undemanding dishes such as fishcakes and chips (£6.95) or Caesar salad (£5.50 as a main course) is generally quite satisfying. This is a key breakfasting spot (£5.90 for the full works) and also ideal for supper before the Royal Court Theatre. House wine is a not inconsiderable £9.95. / 10.30 pm; no smoking area; no booking.

Osteria Antica Bologna SW11 £18 ★
23 Northcote Rd   978 4771   6-2C 285
This small, cramped, rustic Italian restaurant in Clapham has generated quite a name for itself. We wonder if the success is beginning to tell (and on our recent visit the total bill was unexpectedly high), but there's little doubt that the Italian tapas, assaggi (£1.90 to £4.75) and dishes such as pappardelle with sausage ragoût (£5.50) generally please. Meat and fish dishes are around £7 or £8. Best value is the set lunch of two courses for £7.50 – the same cost as a bottle of the house vino. / 11 pm.

Osteria Basilico W11 £16 Ⓐ★
29 Kensington Pk Rd   727 9957   5-1A 286
The only real problem with this trendy, moderately priced Italian restaurant in Notting Hill is that you can never be quite sure that you're going to get in. Still, it's probably worth the risk, as this is a very enjoyable, buzzy place (especially upstairs), serving reliable dishes and offering very good overall value. A typical meal would be to select antipasti from the buffet (£3.95) and follow up with a pasta or risotto (about £5 to £6) or a more substantial dish such as chicken or salmon (£7.50 to £8.50). House wine is £7.20. / 11 pm; no credit cards.

Le Palais du Jardin WC2 £18 Ⓐ★
136 Long Acre   379 5353   3-3C 287
This grand, slickly fitted out Covent Garden brasserie is undoubtedly the most impressive place in the area and brings an unusual degree of glamour to a meal which need not be very expensive. Nearly all the starters are under a fiver – say snails in pastry (£3.95) or chilled langoustine tails (£4.25). To keep costs within our limit, you would do best, for your main course selection, to stick to the cuisine grand-mère section of the (long) menu – you might choose fishcakes (£5.95) or boeuf bourguignon (£6.95). House wine is £8.50. / Midnight.

Park Inn W2 £15 ★
6 Wellington Ter   229 3553   5-2B   288
On Notting Hill Gate (opposite Kensington Gardens), this
friendly Chinese restaurant may offer little in the way of style,
but on the culinary front it's extremely reliable and very good
value. Most dishes on the main menu are around £5 and
Tiger beer is £2.10 a bottle. Lunch is a special bargain, with
£4.30 buying you soup, a main dish with rice, orange
segments and coffee. / 11.30 pm.

Pâtisserie Valerie £5 Ⓐ★
105 Marylebone High St, W1   935 6240   2-1A   289
44 Old Compton St, W1   437 3466   3-2A   290
66 Portland Pl, W1   580 5533   2-1B   291
215 Brompton Rd, SW3   823 9971   4-2C   292
These four pâtisseries may be in common ownership, but they
are, in fact, all very different. The characterful Soho original is
a cakes, coffee and croissant spot and, to our mind, quite
the best place in that part of town to start the day.
In Marylebone, the famous Maison Sagne (only
recently brought into the group) brings a high degree of
frescoed, continental chic to the cake and coffee experience.
That branch also offers a few light snack dishes, as do both
the large branch near Harrods (probably the best all-round
snackery thereabouts) and the new branch at the elegant
Portland Place headquarters of the Royal Institute of
British Architects. / 6 pm-9 pm, Sun earlier (RIBA closed);
W1, no credit cards.

Paulo's W6 £14 ★
30 Greyhound Rd   385 9264   6-1B   293
When you want to fill up on something a little different, try
the £9.50 all-you-can-eat Brazilian buffet, served up cheerfully
by Paulo and his wife in the front room of their Hammersmith
home. It's simple, tasty fare (with lots for vegetarians),
agreeably and efficiently served. There are starters and
puddings for around £2. House wine is £7.50. Ring the
lower bell of the door on the left. / 10.30 pm; D only;
closed Sun; no credit cards.

The Peasant EC1 £19 ★
240 St John's St   336 7726   7-3D   294
This converted pub, situated just south of the Angel, offers a
relatively short menu of fashionable Mediterranean fare.
Polenta fritters or a spinach, watercress and coriander
salad (both £4.50) are typical of the starters, and you might
have Sicilian stew (£7.50) or roast rabbit (£9) to follow.
House wine is £8.50. The place has quite a hip following,
perhaps explaining why the staff sometimes give the
impression that they regard prompt service as uncool.
/ 10.45 pm; closed Sat L & Sun; no Amex.

Pélican WC2 £19 Ⓐ
45 St Martin's Ln   379 0309   3-4C 295

*Sheer scale adds a feeling of glamour to this recently
revamped Theatreland brasserie. The Gallic staples – this is
effectively the flagship of the Café Rouge chain – are not the
main attraction, but the place is a useful haven in the area. At
lunch and until 7.30pm, they offer a two course meal for
£9.95. On Sunday, there is a brunch menu with the likes of
oeufs Florentine or asparagus omelette (both around a fiver)
or roast beef with Yorkshire pud (£8.95). House wine
is £8.75. / 12.30 am, Sun 10.30 pm.*

The People's Palace SE1 £18 Ⓐ★★
South Bank Centre   928 9999   2-3D 296

*Opened just before we went to press, the huge new dining
room at the Royal Festival Hall may become something of a
London landmark. Its advantages include a great view, gutsy
modern British cooking (overseen by celeb' chef Gary Rhodes)
and prices, which (if they hold) offer excellent value. The two
course set menu is £10.50 (and you would probably want at
least one veg, £1.80). House wine is £9 and coffee £2. You
might have chunky tomato soup, followed by cod on mashed
potato with pear tart to finish. The only negative is the slightly
institutional décor of the Festival Hall (the singular carpet, for
instance), but they have made efforts to overcome this feeling,
and, for a meal before or after a concert, this is certainly a
top choice. / 11 pm.*

Le P'tit Normand SW18 £18 ★
185 Merton Rd   0181-871 0233   6-2B 297

*This Southfields spot is one of the few establishments in
London that might really pass for an unpretentious local
restaurant in France. Though the quality level is high, even à
la carte, prices are reasonable – fish soup (£3.35), fillet of
pork with honey (£8.75). Even better value, though, can be
had from the three course set lunch (£9.95, £11.95
on Sunday). House wine is £7.95. / 10 pm, Sat 11 pm;
closed Sat L; no Switch.*

Phoenicia W8 £14* ★
11-13 Abingdon Rd   937 0120   4-1A 298

*They're rightly proud of their £9.95 buffet lunch at this family-
run Lebanese restaurant in Kensington. The meal consists of
about 40 dishes, including meze, some more substantial
items and also coffee. The house wine is £9.45. You could,
with a degree of care, dine here within our price limit.
/ 11.45 pm.*

Pierre Victoire   **£ 15**   –
6 Panton St, SW1   930 6463   3-4A   ²⁹⁹
9 William St, SW1   823 2070   2-3A   ³⁰⁰
29-31 Foubert's Pl, W1   439 2557   2-2B   ³⁰¹
294 Fulham Rd, SW10   795 0048   4-3B   ³⁰²
71 New Broadway, W5   0181-840 0050   1-2A   ³⁰³
22 Golders Green Rd, NW11   0181-731 7406   1-1B   ³⁰⁴
2 Canfield Gnds, NW6   372 3431   7-1B   ³⁰⁵
136 Upper R'mnd Rd, SW15   0181-789 7043   6-2B   ³⁰⁶
Ramshackle domesticity is the theme of these French inspired
budget bistros. Standards are not consistent, but, especially
with their £4.90 three course set lunch (changing daily at
every branch), you can eat a nutritious if not exciting meal
very reasonably. It's quite a lot more expensive à la carte.
House wine is £6.15 a bottle. / 11 pm; SW15 closed Sun; no Amex.

Pitcher & Piano   **£ 14**   Ⓐ
70 Dean St, W1   434 3585   3-2A   ³⁰⁷
40-42 King William IV St, WC2   240 6180   3-4C   ³⁰⁸
214 Fulham Rd, SW10   352 9234   4-3B   ³⁰⁹
871-873 Fulham Rd, SW6   736 3910   6-1B   ³¹⁰
18-20 Chiswick High Rd, W4   0181-742 7731   1-3A   ³¹¹
On Friday nights they queue down the street to get into the
huge, extremely successful branch near Trafalgar Square of
this chain of bars. All are crowded rendezvous, popular with
twentysomethings for a night out. The food on offer –
undemanding dishes for around a fiver – is far from being the
main point of the places, but it's perfectly competently done.
House wine is £9.50. The new, Soho branch is a useful
addition. / 10 pm-11 pm; W1 closed Sun.

Pizza Chelsea SW3   **£ 13**   –
93 Pelham St   584 4788   4-2C   ³¹²
Worn out by your exertions at Conran?, jaded by Joseph?,
ground down by Gaultier? – if you're looking for a reasonably
priced meal around Brompton Cross, you might consider this
comfortable and chic (if perhaps slightly sterile) spot.
Pizzas are priced from £5.25 to £6.95, and the house
wine is £8.50. / 11 pm; no smoking area.

Pizza On The Park SW1   **£ 12**   Ⓐ★
11 Knightsbridge   235 5550   2-3A   ³¹³
The grandest of all the PizzaExpresses (see also) has large,
light and airy premises near Hyde Park Corner, and boasts a
menu which is both a fraction more expensive than usual
(with pizzas around £6) and more extensive, including
breakfast (full works, £4.95). House wine is £8.
Downstairs there is a major jazz and cabaret venue
(substantial music charge). / Midnight; no smoking area; no booking.

Pizza Pomodoro   £15   A
51 Beauchamp Pl, SW3   589 1278   4-1C   314
7 Steward St, E1   377 6186   8-1D   315
110 Old St, EC1   250 0544   8-1B   316
*The original Pomodoro, in a cramped and seedy Knightsbridge
basement is one of London's top late places – with live music
and a positively Latin atmosphere. Pizzas there are about £6
and the house wine is £10 a bottle. The City branches, if not
quite as characterful, are good in their way, and a little less
expensive. / SW3 1 am, City, 11pm-Midnight; City closed Sat & Sun.*

Pizza the Action SW6   £12   A★
678 Fulham Rd   736 2716   6-1B   317
*Ever-popular, welcoming, all-day Fulham bistro, which would
be a welcome addition to any area. With most starters
around £3, and the cheapest pizzas only a fraction more, it
really isn't expensive – the priciest dish on the wide-ranging
menu is a rib-eye steak and chips (£7.50). House wine
is £6.95. / Midnight; no Switch.*

PizzaExpress   £10   A★
10 Dean St, W1   437 9595   2-2C   318
21-22 Barrett St, W1   629 1001   2-2A   319
29 Wardour St, W1   437 7215   3-3A   320
30 Coptic St, WC1   636 3232   2-1C   321
9-12 Bow St, WC2   240 3443   3-2D   321a
363 Fulham Rd, SW10   352 5300   4-3B   322
895 Fulham Rd, SW6   731 3117   6-1B   323
137 Notting Hl Gt, W11   229 6000   5-2B   324
7 Rockley Rd, W14   0181-749 8582   1-3B   325
26 Porchester Rd, W2   229 7784   5-1C   326
252 Chiswick High Rd, W4   0181-747 0193   1-3A   327
23 Bond St, W5   0181-567 7690   1-2A   328
35 Earl's Ct Rd, W8   937 0761   4-1A   329
335 Upper St, N1   226 9542   7-3D   330
94 Golders Gn Rd, NW11   0181-455 9556   1-1B   331
194 Haverstock Hill, NW3   794 6777   7-2A   332
227 Finchley Rd, NW3   794 5100   1-1B   333
Chapter Ho, Montague Cl, SE1   378 6446   8-3C   334
70 Westow Hl, SE19   0181-670 1786   1-4C   335
230 Lavender Hl, SW11   223 5677   6-2C   336
46 Battersea Br Rd, SW11   924 2774   6-1C   337
305 Up R'mnd Rd W, SW14   0181-878 6833   6-2A   338
144 Up R'mnd Rd, SW15   0181-789 1948   6-2B   339
539 Old York Rd, SW18   0181-877 9812   6-2B   340
84 High St, SW19   0181-946 6027   6-2B   341
*For years now, we've been singing the praises of this chain of
reliable, stylish, reasonably priced pizzerias – and thankfully
there's no reason to change that opinion. Pizzas are priced
from £3.40 to £6.15, and house wine is £7.60. Their new
branch, right by the Royal Opera House, conclusively
demonstrates that budget dining can be chic – other popular
branches are Coptic Street (near the British Museum) and
Wardour Street in Soho. Coming soon – Beauchamp Place
and Baker Street. / 11 pm-Midnight; (Chapter Hse 4.30 pm and closed
Sat & Sun); booking at some branches only.*

Pizzeria Castello SE1 £ 10 A ★
20 Walworth Rd   703 2556   1-3C 342
*Its supporters claim this unattractively located pizzeria
(just south of the Elephant and Castle) as the best in London.
That's a moot point, but no one doubts the reliability and
value of the pizzas (£3.60 to £5.60) or pastas (£3.60 to
£4.10). House wine is £6.90. There is live music every
night except Friday. / 11 pm; closed Sat L & Sun.*

Pizzeria Condotti W1 £ 13 ★
4 Mill St   499 1308   2-2B 343
*It may not give the feeling of being in quite its first flush of
youth, but this Mayfair version of PizzaExpress, near
Hanover Square, still offers fair value for pizzas and salads
(both around £6) and the like in this pricey part of town.
House wine is £8. It's especially popular at weekday
lunchtimes, when it can get rather crowded and smoky.
Sunday lunchtime opening is a recent innovation. / Midnight;
closed Sun D; no Switch.*

The Place Below EC2 £ 10 ★★
St Mary-le-Bow, Cheapside   329 0789   8-2C 344
*One of London's best vegetarian restaurants shelters in the
characterful crypt of St Mary-le-Bow. At lunchtime, it's a bit of
a scrum, with self-service of dishes like carrot and tarragon
soup (£2.30), aubergine and chick pea casserole (£5.75) and
avocado with almond and garlic dressing with roast peppers
(£6.25). On Thursday and Friday nights, though, you can
book for a waiter-served, three course blow-out (£17.50, or
two courses for £15), and BYO. / Mon-Wed L only, Thu and Fri
9.30 pm; closed Sat & Sun; no credit cards; no smoking; book only for eves.*

Planet Hollywood W1 £ 17 A
13 Coventry St   287 1000   3-4A 345
*OK, the food is neither the main attraction nor particularly
cheap at this movie-shrine-cum-burger-restaurant near
Leicester Square. But if you want somewhere with a sense of
occasion, this dramatically decorated space offers a pretty
good package, with something for all the family. A burger or
pizza is £7.95 and the large menu includes similarly priced
pastas, salads and sandwiches as well as some more
expensive grills. A bottle of Becks will set you back £2.15.
/ 1 am; no smoking area; no booking.*

Planet Poppadom SW3 £ 11 A ★
366 King's Rd   823 3368   4-3C 346
*This modestly decorated but fun Indian restaurant in Chelsea
has been a real hit with the younger crowd. Starters are
£2.50 (say a quarter tandoori chicken) and baltis – chicken,
lamb, prawn and vegetarian – are all £4.95. There is also a
selection of tandoori and biryani dishes. Bottled beers are
£2.25. / 11.45 pm; closed L Mon-Fri; no Amex.*

Prost W11 £ 14 ★
35 Pembridge Rd   727 9620   5-2B   368
*This eastern European place, just off Notting Hill Gate, has a
slightly unusual ambience. It's more like an English tea shop
than a restaurant (and, indeed, in the afternoons, they serve
the likes of apple strudel at £2.25 and coffee). The menu
with dishes such as mushrooms filled with blue cheese
(£2.95) and wild boar sausage (£7.95), has no great
pretensions, but the food is solid, tasty and comforting. From
6pm to 8pm they do a very good value two course offer,
whereby you can have a main course with a starter or
pudding for just £7.95. House wine is £8.50. / 11 pm; closed Mon;
no Switch.*

Pucci Pizza SW3 £ 15 𝔸
205 King's Rd   352 2134   4-3C   369
*The competition gets ever hotter, but this tacky Chelsea
pizzeria remains the place where the young and beautiful
hang out while waiting to be discovered. Salads are around
£4.50, pizzas are around £5.50 and the house wine is £8.50.
/ 12.30 am; closed Sun; no credit cards.*

Quaglino's W1 £19* 𝔸★
16 Bury St   930 6767   2-3B   370
*When it opened a couple of years ago, this huge, very
glamorous St James's brasserie was the most significant
restaurant opening in London since the war. Lunchtime or pre-
theatre, you can squeeze a meal within our budget if you
stick to the set three course meal for £12.95 – perhaps
noodles with ginger, followed by confit of duck, with baked
apple and custard to finish. Otherwise, there is always the
option of the antipasto bar overlooking the restaurant, which
offers the possibility of an elegant, if not inexpensive, snack –
they serve dishes such as grilled chicken salad (£6.50).
House wine is £10.95 (£2.95 a glass). There is a 12.5%
service charge throughout. / Midnight, Fri & Sat 1 am; no Switch.*

Le Quai EC4 £ 14 𝔸
1 Broken Whf   236 6480   8-3B   371
*An expense account City lunching restaurant might seem an
odd recommendation for this book, but the bar here (which
overlooks the river) offers a good menu of snacks such as
steak sandwiches or grilled chicken (both £4.50) or grilled
fillet of sole (£8.95). House wine is a hefty £12.50. / 8 pm;
closed Sat & Sun.*

Rani N3   **£ 16**   ★★
7 Long Ln   0181-349 4386   1-1B   372
This very professionally run Indian vegetarian restaurant in
Finchley is one of the best in town. It's far from being one of
the cheapest, however, with set menus in the evening starting
at £12.70 (though on Monday they do a £10 buffet). A nice
touch is the children's set menu (£5.50), which includes a
series of plainer dishes spiced up with that old Indian
speciality, tomato ketchup. Kingfisher is £2.10 a bottle.
Hurrah for the tipping policy – it's not allowed. / 10.30 pm;
D only; closed Sat L; no smoking area.

Ranoush W1   **£ 9**   ★
43 Edgware Rd   723 5929   5-1D   373
Especially for a late night snack, this excellent Middle Eastern
café is a good value (if not hyper-cheap) spot worth
remembering. The standard of the brightly-lit, glitzy décor is
high, as is that of the dips, salads and kebabs (beautifully
done, all for around £3 or less). For a blow-out, they offer a
selection of six meze for £9. They are unlicensed, and don't
accept cheques. / 3 am; no credit cards.

Ransome's Dock SW11   **£17***   A★
35 Parkgate Rd   223 1611   6-1C   374
This rather hidden restaurant, near Battersea Bridge, is one of
the most popular south of the river. Prices at dinner are just
outside our range, but during the week you might like to visit
for the set lunch of two courses (£11.50). That might
comprise mushroom and Madeira soup to start followed by
smoked haddock Florentine. Alternatively, the weekend
brunch menu offers the likes of scrambled eggs and bacon
(£4.60) or Cumberland sausage fry-up (£9). House wine
is £10. / 11 pm; closed Sun D.

Rebato's SW8   **£ 14**   A★
169 South Lambeth Rd   735 6388   6-1D   375
Vauxhall is, rather implausibly, the location of what many vote
London's best tapas bar – authentic all the way down to the
rather macho attitude sometimes adopted by the waiters.
Dishes range from £2 to £4, and the house wine is £7.50.
Alternatively you could go through the bar to the more sedate
restaurant at the rear, where three courses – you might have
calamares, paella and a pudding – will set you back £13.50.
/ 10.30 pm; closed Sat L & Sun; no Switch.

The Red Pepper W9   **£ 13**   ★★
8 Formosa St   266 2708   1-2B   376
Pizzas from one of London's few wood-burning ovens are the
star attraction at this sparsely furnished Mediterranean
Maida Vale spot, which has created for itself one of the
strongest reputations of any of London's recently established
less expensive restaurants. They also do excellent home-made
pasta and delicious specials, such as marinated salmon with
rocket, pine kernels and cherry tomatoes. Most main course
dishes are around £6, and the house wine is £8 a bottle.
It's advisable to book. / 10.45 pm; closed Mon; no Amex.

Ristorante Italiano W1   £ 18   A ★
54 Curzon St   629 2742   2-3B   377
*This elegant restaurant, just by Shepherd Market, attracts
traditionalists of all ages. There's not really anything to
criticise – the setting is light and agreeable, the old-style staff
are efficient and the cooking of simple dishes is often good.
Much of the menu is in the £7 to £9 price range, and, for
economy, there is always the option of pasta as a main
course (£5.75 to £6.75). House wine is £8.* / 11.15 pm;
closed Sat L & Sun; no smoking area.

La Rive Gauche SE1   £ 19   ★
61 The Cut   928 8645   8-4A   378
*The fact that this South Bank French restaurant, a stone's
throw from the Old Vic, is a little conservative and middle-
aged possibly only heightens its appeal to its main customers
– local businessmen and theatre-goers. A la carte, you could
spend quite a lot here, but they offer a good two course set
meal – say vichyssoise and pan-fried lemon sole – for £13.
Unlimited coffee with petits fours is £1.95, and the house
wine £10.50.* / 11 pm; closed Sat L & Sun.

Rock Garden WC2   £ 13   A
6-7 The Piazza, Cov Gdn   836 4052   3-3D   379
*Despite its prime tourist rip-off joint location (overlooking the
Covent Garden piazza), this welcoming burger parlour offers
quite good value – a burger is £5.75, and a bottle of Rolling
Rock £2.50 – and the outside tables have one of the nicest
alfresco locations in town. Downstairs, there is one of
London's longest-surviving rock venues.* / Midnight, Fri & Sat 1 am.

Rock Island Diner W1   £ 14   A
2nd Fl London Pavilion   287 5500   2-2C   380
*Although it feels like somewhere between a burger diner and
a theme park – the staff periodically jump on the tables and
sing numbers from 'Grease' – this very centrally located place
attracts a surprisingly broad following. Part of the reason may
be that the burgers (£6.25, with fries and garnish) are
actually quite good, or you could choose a salad (not of the
particularly healthy sort) for around £7. There's a range of
American beers at £2.50. Till 5pm on Saturday and Sunday,
a kid eats free with each adult ordering a main course.*
/ 11.30 pm; no booking.

Rodos WC2   £ 12   ★
59 St Giles High St   836 3177   3-1B   381
*Neither outside (nestling beside Centre Point) nor inside is this
a place of beauty, but this long-established, family-owned
Greek restaurant has many followers for the quality of its
traditional-style cooking. The notably good taramasalata is
£2.65, dolmades (stuffed vine leaves) £2.95 and stifado
(beef stew) £5.85. The house wine is £7.90.* / 11.15 pm;
closed Sat L & Sun; no Switch.

Rôtisserie W12   **£ 18**   A ★
56 Uxbridge Rd   0181-743 3028   1-3B   382
Protein-lovers should make a beeline for the £8.95 menu
always available at this welcoming Shepherd's Bush restaurant
– soup, salad, or starter of the day, followed by steak,
chicken, moules or fish, with frites. A la carte,
you would spent quite a lot more. The house wine is
£8.95 a bottle. As we go to press, a new branch is to open at
134 Upper Street N1. / 11 pm, Fri & Sat 11.30 pm; closed Sat L & Sun.

Rôtisserie Jules SW7   **£ 9**   –
6-8 Bute St   584 0600   4-2B   383
The speciality of this small, elegantly designed canteen in
South Kensington is flame-grilled, free-range chicken (quarter
bird with frites or salad, £4.95). Groups of between five and
eight might like to order a gigot d'agneau (£17 to £25,
depending on weight). At the time of writing, you should BYO
(£1.50 corkage), but a licence has been applied for. Another
change afoot is a new branch under construction at
338 King's Road SW3. / 11.30 pm; no credit cards.

Royal China   **£10*** A ★★
13 Queensway, W2   221 2535   5-2C   384
3 Chelverton Rd, SW15   0181-788 0907   6-2B   385
Glamorous in a deeply '70s way, these black and gold oriental
restaurants in Bayswater and Putney are among the best of
their type in London. In the evenings, you would have to
scrimp rather to stay within our price range, but there are no
such problems at lunchtime, when dim sum (£1.60 to £2.90)
offer the prospect of a delicious and interesting lunch (and in
comfortable surroundings) for under a tenner. / 11.15 pm;
no booking Sun L.

Ruby in the Dust   **£ 14**   A
70 Upper St, N1   359 1710   7-3D   386
102 Camden High St, NW1   485 2744   7-3C   387
110 St John's Hill, SW11   223 8708   6-2B   388
These atmospheric, dimly lit places in Camden Town, Islington
and (most recently) Clapham are worth remembering for
their buzzy atmosphere – ideal for budget parties – rather
than for any culinary excitement. Typical dishes are 'skins'
(£3.95), home-made burgers (£5.95) and Creole chicken
(£6.45), and there is a wide list of drinks – a jug of sangria
(£8.95), bottled beers (£2.35), cocktails (£3.50) and a
number of shots. (If you want to finish your party late,
Islington boasts a bar open till 2am – small entry charge).
/ 11.15 pm; SW11, Mon-Fri closed L; no Amex.

Rueda SW4   **£ 12**   A
66-68 Clapham High St   627 2173   6-2D   389
There is frankly nothing very special about the tapas (£2.60
to £4.50) at this famous Clapham bar, whose authenticity is
aided by a decorative scheme that consists almost entirely of
Spanish wine bottles. As an atmospherically fun place,
however, it has few equals. House wine is £7.50.
/ 11 pm; book only in restaurant.

Rules WC2   £19*   A★★

35 Maiden Ln   836 5314   3-3D   390

Rules claims to be the oldest restaurant in London, and, with its beautiful panelled interior, it is undoubtedly one of the most charming. Usually, it's an expense account type of place. If you're prepared to eat at 'off-peak' times, however, you can have practically the run of the menu – and it's a long and varied one – at remarkably low cost. For your two courses, you might choose, for example, to have smoked salmon followed by roast quail, or perhaps a rump steak. This will cost you ONLY £7.95 on a weekday afternoon (3pm-5pm). As an early pre-theatre meal (order by 6pm, Mon-Fri) or at the weekends (noon-4pm) the price for two courses is £12.95, which is still amazingly good value. House wine is £8.50 a bottle, and coffee £1.75. Hurry, hurry, hurry – this one may not last! / 11.30 pm.

S&P SW3   £18   ★

181 Fulham Rd   351 5692   4-2C   391

Menu details here are as for S&P Patara (below). It's a place equally worth knowing about in its area. / 10.30 pm.

S&P Patara SW3   £18   ★

9 Beauchamp Pl   581 8820   4-1C   392

You can find spectacularly bad value restaurants among the chichi shops of Beauchamp Place. Not here, though, where enjoyable Thai food is graciously served in pretty (if fairly tightly packed) surroundings. The set lunches (£7.95 or £9.95) provide a pleasant break from consumerism and offer the best value, but you can also keep within our price range in the evening. Singha beer is £2.50. / 10.30 pm; no smoking area.

Sarcan N1   £13   ★

4 Theberton St   226 5489   7-3D   393

A very smart and welcoming place by the standards of kebab houses, this friendly dining room, just off Islington's Upper Street, offers tasty dishes and good value. For two or more people, set meals are available, consisting of a selection of starters and kebabs, together with a pudding and coffee, for £9.95 per head. A kebab on its own is about a fiver. There's also a good range of Middle Eastern vegetarian dishes at around £4 each. House wine is £7. / Midnight; no Amex & no Switch.

Sash SW6   £11   A★

825 Fulham Rd   736 9429   6-1B   394

Though a relative newcomer, this oriental 'tapas' bar in Fulham is already attracting a good following. We suspect that it's the jolly (chaotic, if you prefer) atmosphere which is the principal attraction, but the food is by no means bad and you can eat here at relatively little cost. For example, at lunchtime, you can have three courses for £5.95. In the evening, there's just the tapas menu, from which Thai soup is £2.75 and Indonesian fish curry is £3.75. The house wine is £6.75 (or £5 during the happy hour from 5.30pm to 8pm). / 11 pm; no Switch.

Savoy Group August Offer
*London's most pukka group of hotels generally does some sort
of special promotion during the month of August. (Well what
are you to do if all your customers are on the grouse moors?)
An unusual advantage of the 1995 offer is that it will run
from midday to midnight, seven days a week – so book
ahead for that 8.30pm table! A £12 menu will be
available not only at Claridge's Causerie (2 courses), but also
at the Brasserie and the Grill St Quentin (both 3 courses),
and at Simpsons-in-the-Strand (2 courses). See the individual
entries for contact details.*

The Scarsdale W8   £14   A
23a Edwardes Sq   937 1811   4-2A   395
*This pretty, flower-bedecked pub overlooks one of
Kensington's oldest and most attractive squares, and the main
problem is that it's often difficult to find anywhere to sit, either
inside or in the tiny garden. The food is a little more ambitious
than usual pub grub, and well done. It might include dishes
like beef and stilton pie or Cajun butterfly chicken
(both £6.25). The Sunday roast (and three veg)
costs £5.95. Theakstons bitter is £1.82 per pint.*
/ 9.30 pm; no Amex & no Switch.

Seashell NW1   £15   ★
49 Lisson Gr   723 8703   7-4A   396
*It is claimed that the burghers of north London regularly
despatch their chauffeurs to collect fish and chips from this
celebrated shop. Whether this is really justified is open to
question, but you can see that this is no ordinary chippie.
In the dining room, cod and chips will set you back £7.95.
Best value is the three course set menu – soup, fish of the
day with chips, ice cream and tea or coffee for £9.50,
available from noon to 2pm, and from 5pm to 7pm. House
wine is £8.95.* / 10.15 pm; closed Sun D; no smoking area; no booking.

The Shampan E1   £13   ★
79 Brick Ln   375 0475   1-2D   397
*This smart but soulless restaurant is one of the best on this
famous East End street packed with curry-houses. It may not
be the cheapest in the area, but it offers very good value. The
most expensive option is the tandoori prawn biryani (£8.95),
but most things, including balti dishes, are around half that
price. A large bottle of Cobra is £3.55.* / Midnight.

Shampers W1   £13   A
4 Kingly St   437 1692   2-2B   398
*This bubbly Soho wine bar is a popular and convivial place.
The food is not remarkable, but there's a good range of wine
bar dishes, such as squid salad or ham and cheese pie (both
£5.50). At lunchtime, you can also eat more substantial fare
in the downstairs restaurant, perhaps grilled aubergine with
pesto (£3.50) followed by home made duck sausages with
lentils (£8.95). House wine is £9.50.* / 11 pm; closed Sat D & Sun.

Shaw's SW7 £20* A ★★
399

119 Old Brompton Rd   373 7774   4-2B

This rather stuffy South Kensington establishment (on the site of the former Chanterelle bistro) has achieved instant acclaim for its modern British cooking. At most times it is well beyond our budget, but they offer a very good value £14 two course meal (including coffee) both for weekday lunch and also after 10.30pm. The dishes are exotic for a menu of this type – you might choose a salad of air-dried duck and then grilled brill with scallops, lobster and spicy lentils. House wine is £13.50 a bottle (£3 a glass). / 11.30 pm; closed Sat L & Sun D.

Shillibeer's N7 £17 A ★
400

Carpenter's Mews, North Rd   700 1858   7-2C

The scale and style of this place on the Kentish Town/Islington border seems much more American than European – apart from the burgers (£5.95) on the bar menu, however, there's not much transatlantic influence on the menu. For example, if you had the £10.95 three course menu in the restaurant, you might have seafood torte, stuffed sole, and strawberry shortcake. Saturday night, when they generally go on till 2am, is cabaret night, and there's a £15 set menu, including the music charge. House wine is £8. / 11 pm.

The Ship SW18 £12 A ★
401

Jews Rw   0181-870 9667   6-2B

This excellent Wandsworth establishment boasts a large riverside yard and gets incredibly crowded on a warm day. Generally, the food is above pub standards (and a restaurant area has recently been added), but the top attraction is their summer charcoal barbecue (where meaty dishes are priced at up to a tenner). Dishes on the standard menu range from pastas of the day (around £4) to venison bangers and mash (£5.10). Young's bitter is £1.70 a pint, but they are also keen to stress their selection of 20 wines available by the glass. / 10 pm.

Le Shop SW3 £11 A
402

329 King's Rd   352 3891   4-3C

Chelsea's 'Véritable Crêperie' (as it styles itself) is a well established haunt for those looking for a snack meal in this pricey part of town – savoury pancakes are about £5, and sweet ones a little less. Assuming loud classical music is to your taste, the ambience is agreeable. House wine is £6.95. At the time of writing, a 'recession' lunch menu – a pancake, side salad and glass of wine – is still available for £5. / Midnight; no Amex & no Switch.

Shree Krishna SW17 £13 ★
403

192-194 Tooting High St   0181-672 4250   6-2C

Beautiful it is not, but this Tooting South Indian restaurant has a justified reputation for the quality of its cooking. The speciality (mainly vegetarian) dishes are priced between £1.80 and £4 and curries are about £3.50. Kingfisher is £2.20 a pint. / Mon-Thu 10.45 pm, Fri & Sat 11.45 pm; no Switch.

Simpson's of Lloyds Avenue EC3   £14   ★

Lloyds Av   481 1168   8-3D   404

The City is still rather short of places where a quality light meal can be had at reasonable cost. Formerly called Marlows, this slightly odd establishment – half cafeteria, half wine bar – fills the gap nicely. The simple dishes such as sandwiches (£3.95), the roast of the day (£6.95) or salads (£5.95) are well done. House wine is £8.25. / L only; closed Sat & Sun; no smoking area.

Simpson's of Cornhill EC3   £12   Ⓐ★★

38 1/2 Cornhill   626 9985   8-2C   405

Little has changed at this back alley City chop-house since Dickens's day (he is reputed to have been a customer) and the daily crush of bankers and brokers wouldn't have it any other way. The food is magnificently unfashionable, and is strong on chops (£4.30) and steaks (£5.90), bubble and squeak (£1.20), and even savouries – stewed cheese is £1.85. House wine is £9.95 a litre. / L only; closed Sat & Sun; no booking.

Simpsons-in-the-Strand WC2   £16*   Ⓐ★

100 Strand   836 9112   3-3D   406

Simpson's is more than just a restaurant – it is THE great traditional English restaurant, famous for its huge weekly consumption of sides of beef. It's a grand and characterful place, and generally, quite pricey. However, they do a two course £10 menu, which is available at weekday lunchtimes and between 6pm and 6.30pm. The evening (and Friday lunch) menus even include the famous beef, offering exceptional value. Alternatively, for £10.50, you can start the day with a big fry-up – they serve till noon, so have a late breakfast and skip lunch. House wine is £12. / 11 pm; no Switch.

Singapore Garden NW6   £16   ★

82-83A Fairfax Rd   328 5314   7-2A   407

The décor may be a touch on the tacky side, but this Swiss Cottage restaurant attracts a broad following with the quality of its wide-ranging oriental menu, mixing Indonesian, Thai and Chinese dishes. You might start with fishball soup (£2.50), and follow it up with Szechuan crispy beef (£5.50) or perhaps Ho Jien (oyster omelette Singapore style, £7.60). House wine is £8.50. / 10.45 pm.

606 Club SW10   £ 18   𝔸 ★
90 Lots Rd   352 5953   4-4B   **408**
You might not expect the food in a trendy cellar jazz-joint
(through a hole in a wall, opposite the Lots Road Power
Station) to be up to much. Fortunately – although it has no
very great aspirations – this is not the case, and dishes such
as grilled prawns (£4.25) or shepherd's pie (£5.20) are done
with care. After the £4 (or so) music charge, you will have to
be careful to stay within our price limit, but you do, after all,
get your entertainment thrown in. Someone must think it's a
good deal as the place has recently expanded to meet
demand. House wine is £8.20. / Mon-Thu 1.30 am, Fri & Sat 2 am,
Sun 11.30 pm; D only; no Amex.

Smokey Joe's SW18   £ 9   ★
131 Wandsworth High St   0181-871 1785   6-2B   **409**
The size of this microscopic Wandsworth diner gives little
clue to the breadth of its reputation for good soul cooking.
Starters (such as stuffed plantains or peppered prawns) are
about £3, and main dishes (such as barbecued ribs or jerk
pork) about £6. It's a perfectly pleasant place and you can
BYO (no corkage), but it's not really designed to encourage
you to linger for very long. / 10 pm; closed Sun L; no credit cards; no
booking.

Smollensky's on the Strand WC2   £ 16   𝔸
105 The Strand   497 2101   3-3D   **410**
This grandly fitted out American theme restaurant in the
Strand claims its £10.45 special fixed price menu is 'the best
steak offer in London'. We think they may be right –
it includes a choice of starters, a rib-eye steak and chips,
steak sauce, and a glass of wine or beer, or a soft drink.
Other dishes, salade Niçoise (£6.95) for example, are not
quite so attractively priced, but the place is rightly known for
the great efforts it makes to keep the kids happy at
weekends. It also offers music nightly, with a DJ (Thu-Sat).
House wine is £8.60. / Midnight, Fri & Sat , Thu 12.30 am, Sun 10 pm;
no smoking area.

Snows on the Green W6   £17*   ★★
166 Shepherd's Bush Rd   603 2142   1-3B   **411**
This bright (perhaps too bright) modern restaurant in
Brook Green continues to establish its reputation for
innovative Mediterranean cooking. It's within our price limit at
lunch only, when they do set menus of two (£11.50) or three
(£13.50) courses. You might have duck and lentil terrine,
followed by confit of lamb and prune, and ending with an
armagnac tart. House wine is £9.50. / 11 pm;
closed Sat L & Sun D; no Amex.

Sofra £ 18 A★

18 Shepherd St, W1   493 3320   2-3B

412

36 Tavistock St, WC2   240 3773   3-3D

413

Reliability and value are the hallmarks of these Turkish restaurants in Shepherd Market (where there are some excellent outside tables) and in Covent Garden. You might opt for the 'healthy' set menu of Middle Eastern meze (£8.45 at lunch, £9.45 in the evening) or choose from the lengthy à la carte menu at slightly greater cost. The house wine is £9.95. (See also Café Sofra.) / Midnight; W1 no Switch.

Soho Soho W1 £ 19 A★

11-13 Frith St   494 3491   3-2A

414

Cramped and noisy, but vibrant and fun, this rôtisserie/brasserie in central (yes, you guessed it) Soho is one of the more consistent performers and a popular West End rendezvous. You could spend over our limit without undue difficulty, but with dishes like fish soup at £3.50 and spit roast guinea fowl at £9.75, it is just about possible to keep within it. House wine is £9.50. No booking. / rotisserie 12.45 am, restaurant 11.45 pm; rotisserie closed Sun, restaurant closed Sat L & Sun; no smoking area; no booking in rotisserie.

Sonny's SW13 £ 19 A★★

94 Church Rd   0181-748 0393   6-1A

415

A byword for value throughout south west London, this buzzy modern British establishment has always seemed slightly out of place in sleepy old Barnes. A la carte, it's a little out of our price range, but there is always a two course menu available for £13.50, including coffee – you might choose terrine of char-grilled vegetables followed by boned leg of rabbit. There is also (just on the border of our budget) an excellent value three course Sunday lunch for £16.50. House wine is £8.75. An adjoining café (open from 10.30am to 6pm) offers a range of light dishes, few of which are over a fiver. A new Sonny's is scheduled to open in Putney in late 1995. / 11 pm; closed Sun D; no Switch.

Soulard N1 £ 17 ★

113 Mortimer Rd   254 1314   1-1C

416

If you were to imagine a small, cramped bistro in a French provincial town, you might come up with something not very different from this spot on the Hackney/Islington fringe. The fare – perhaps artichoke salad (£3.65) followed by poached cod with basil sauce (£9.20) – is consistently good. House wine is £8.50. / 10.30 pm; D only, closed Sun & Mon; no Switch.

South Bank Brasserie SE1 £ 17 A

Gabriel's Wharf, 56 Upp Ground   620 0596   8-3A

417

The cooking at this riverside brasserie has no particular pretensions, but the realisation of dishes such as salmon fishcakes (£3.95) and marinated fillet of lamb (£8.95) is perfectly competent. The particular attraction, though, is the panoramic view of the City and St Paul's – especially at night, it's one of the best in London. House wine is £7.95. / 11.30 pm; no Switch.

Spago SW7 £11 ★
418

6 Glendower Pl   225 2407   4-2C

Value for money is the watch-word at this unpretentious South
Kensington pizza and pasta stop, where the dishes
(all under £6) almost invariably satisfy. Décor-wise, it's an
unremarkable place, and the more atmospheric front section
is to be preferred to the echoey rear. House wine is £6.80.
/ 11.30 pm; no credit cards.

Sri Siam W1 £18 ★★
419

14 Old Compton St   434 3544   3-2A

This is rightly one of the best known Thai restaurants in
central London. An agreeable place (if, as with most West
End places, rather impersonal in feel), it has good service.
The food, though, is what really impresses, and sometimes
delights. There are set menus at £10.50 (lunch only) and
£15.50, or you can go à la carte for about the same cost.
Singha beer is £2.50. / 11.15 pm; closed Sun L.

Standard Tandoori W2 £12 ★
420

27 Westbourne Gro   229 0600   5-1C

Although it's not nearly as well known as its more frenetic
neighbour, Khan's, this large Bayswater Indian restaurant
offers rather better overall value. It's a civilised, if unexciting,
place, but the level of cooking it offers is well above that
which the name suggests. Most of the main dishes are
under a fiver, and a large bottle of Cobra is £3.50.
/ 11.45 pm; no Switch.

Star Café W1 £4 –
421

22b Gt Chapel St   437 8778   2-2C

Soho is surprisingly short of places for a good greasy
breakfast, and this is the number 1 recommendation
thereabouts. It's a pleasant, rather hidden away place,
offering the full works for £3.95. At lunch, they offer toasted
sandwiches and baps, as well as more substantial hot dishes,
for around a fiver. / L only; closed Sat & Sun; no credit cards; no booking.

The Stepping Stone SW8 £18 A★
422

123 Queenstown Rd   622 0555   6-1C

This understated but welcoming modern British newcomer in
Battersea has already generated quite a following. In the
evening, with dishes such as ricotta tart (£4) and home-made
sausages (£7.75), it's quite possible to enjoy a satisfying meal
reasonably inexpensively. Even more so at lunch, when there's
a set menu for £10.50. On Sundays, the set menu is £11.50
at both lunch and dinner. House wine is £8.50. / 11 pm;
no Switch; no smoking area.

Sticky Fingers W8 £14 ^A
9 Phillimore Gdns   938 5338   4-1A   423
The buzzy atmosphere is the particular strength of this popular American-style Kensington diner, which is owned by Rolling Stones guitarist Bill Wyman, and decorated with his pop memorabilia. The fare is reasonable – burgers and chips (£5.95), and salads and sandwiches at around the same price. Holsten export is £2.30 per pint. / 11.30 pm; book L only.

Stock Pot £7 ★
40 Panton St, SW1   839 5142   3-4A   424
18 Old Compton St, W1   287 1066   3-2B   425
50 James St, W1   486 1086   2-2A   426
273 King's Rd, SW3   823 3175   4-3C   427
6 Basil St, SW3   589 8627   4-1D   428
No one would ever pretend that these basic, '60s-style bistro-cafés offer huge culinary excitement. That said, generations of young Londoners know that they offer reliable standards and low, low prices – it's not so long ago that everything was priced to the nearest penny. The old-fashioned international menu extends from soups (80p), through omelettes (£2.50) and casseroles (£2.75) to fruit crumble (90p), and set menus are often offered at less than a fiver. House wine is £6.50.
/ 11 pm-11.45 pm; no credit cards.

Street Hawker W9 £9* ★
166 Randolph Ave   286 3869   7-4A   429
During the daytime, you get very good value from the set menus (£3.50 to £6.45) at this rather unatmospheric Maida Vale restaurant (situated right by the tube), where the cooking is themed around oriental street food. After 7.30pm, the inexpensive set menus are not available and a meal here costs considerably more. Tiger beer is £2. / 11.15 pm.

Sumos W6 £14 ★
169 King St   0181-741 7916   1-3B   430
Though this inconspicuous Hammersmith Japanese café is hardly an exciting place, it offers a solid package of friendly service, good quality dishes and reasonable prices. At lunch they offer a number of bento box meals with rice, miso soup, seaweed and a main dish (which might be chicken for the £5.90 box, up to sushi, sashimi or tempura for the £10.90 one). At dinner, there are some set meals for around £12. Sapporo beer is £2 a bottle. / 10.45 pm; closed Sat L & Sun; no credit cards.

Topkapi W1　　　　　　　£ 14　　★

25 Marylebone High St　486 1872　2-1A　　456

This rather worn Marylebone Turkish establishment is one of
the better inexpensive options in the immediate vicinity.
Starters are about £2.50, and the kebabs and grills £6 to £8
– but the best value option is the de luxe set Turkish meal,
comprising mixed meze, a mixed grill, sweets and a coffee
for £12.50. House wine is £6.50. / 11.30 pm; no Switch.

Topsy-Tasty W4　　　　　£ 12　　★★

5 Station Parade　0181-995 3407　1-3A　　457

As at its sibling establishment – the rather better known
Bedlington Café – the cooking packs quite a punch at this
slightly smarter Thai restaurant by Chiswick station. Prices are
only marginally higher than at the Bedlington and prices are
similarly kept low by the fact that you can BYO for nominal
corkage. They are licensed, however, with house wine priced
£6 and a bottle of Singha at £2.05. / 10.30 pm; D only; closed Sun;
no credit cards.

Troubadour SW5　　　　£ 8　　Ⓐ

265 Old Brompton Rd　No tel　4-3A　　458

London is short of places where you can linger for an hour
over a cappuccino. This bohemian Earl's Court spot is
probably the most atmospheric coffee-house in town. The
food is competent enough, but the menu is limited to dishes
such as omelettes and spaghetti (both £3.90) and cakes
(for about £1). They also do quite a good cooked breakfast
between 10.30am and 12.30pm. No alcohol. / 10.30 pm;
no credit cards; no booking.

Tsukushi NW1　　　　　£ 10　　★

11 Kentish Town Rd　267 1086　7-3B　　459

Close to the tube, this simple Camden Town Japanese café is
a good choice, whether you want a cheap and cheerful place
to linger or just a pleasant place to fill up. There is a variety
of bento boxes from £5.80 (for chicken teriyaki) to £7.50
(for salmon teriyaki or deep fried beef). In addition to the
main dish the box includes pickles, marinated vegetables,
miso soup and rice. BYO – no corkage. / 10 pm; closed Sun;
no credit cards.

Tuk Tuk N1　　　　　　£ 12　　★

330 Upper St　226 0837　7-3D　　460

This simple, minimalist Thai café is ideal for a cheap and
cheerful meal in Islington. The short menu features familiar
dishes – satay (£3.50), spicy red chicken curry and rice
(£5.50) – done to a good standard. A bottle of Singha
beer is £2.50. / 11 pm; closed Sat L & Sun L.

Turner's SW3 £17* A★★

87-89 Walton St   584 6711   4-2C   461

This rather chichi restaurant in what is arguably London's most fashionable restaurant street offers lunches of exceptional value. Two courses cost only £9.95 (or three for £13.50, including service). You might start with lamb's kidney in Madeira sauce, followed by roast guinea fowl stuffed with pâté and, if you went all the way, pear and frangipani tart for pudding. At dinner time, you'd easily blow this book's budget three times over. House wine is £13.50. / 11.15 pm; closed Sat L.

Twenty Trinity Gardens SW9 £18 –

20 Trinity Gdns   733 8838   6-2D   462

Brixton's only modern British establishment offers pretty reliable value. They offer a number of set meals with two courses for £12.75 or £14.95 and there are also some slightly pricier three course options. House wine is £8.95. / 10.30 pm, Fri & Sat 11 pm; D only, closed Sun; no Amex; no smoking area.

Up All Night SW10 £12 –

325 Fulham Rd   352 1996   4-3B   463

There's absolutely nothing remarkable about this Chelsea diner – apart, that is, from the fact that it's open until 6am – well after all the other local establishments (the Earl's Court kebab houses aside) have long ago put up the shutters. The food is very, very ordinary, including staples such as corn on the cob (£2.50) and burgers (£4.80). House wine (in the unlikely event you chose the place during licensed hours) is £7.90. / 6 am; no Amex & no Switch; no booking.

Upper Street Fish Shop N1 £13 A★

324 Upper St   359 1401   7-2D   464

If your idea of a perfect supper is grilled fish and a bottle of Chablis, a chippie might seem an unlikely suggestion. However, this Islington institution has much more the feeling of a bistro, and its fish cooking extends far beyond stodgy standard dishes. A seafood platter, for example, is around a tenner and you can BYO (no corkage). Standard fish and (not so brilliant) chips cost around £7, and traditional English puddings, such as Bakewell tart, are around £2. / 10 pm; closed Mon L & Sun; no Switch; no booking.

Upstairs at the Basil Street SW3 £10 ★

8 Basil St   581 3311   4-1D   465

Fantastically outdated and utterly wonderful hotel carvery and buffet, which dispenses satisfying nosh to a surprisingly chic Knightsbridge crowd – well, perhaps not so surprisingly as the place is just a few paces from Harrods and Harvey Nics. The hot roast of the day is £4.60 and the help-yourself cold buffet £4.35. House wine weighs in at £6.50. / L only; closed Sun; no Switch; no smoking area.

Wine & Kebab SW10   £ 13   –
343 Fulham Rd   352 0967   4-3B   ⁴⁷⁵

If you're looking for real food (as opposed to fast food) in fashionable Chelsea, the choice within our price range is rather meagre. It includes this long-established Greek restaurant, recently redecorated, which now offers quite a good all-round experience – especially if you want to have dinner in the early hours. Start with a mini mezedes (£6.50 for two), and then perhaps moussaka or char-grilled swordfish (each £7). House wine is £7.90. / 2 am; D only.

Wine Gallery   £ 14   𝔸
49 Hollywood Rd, SW10   352 7572   4-3B   ⁴⁷⁶
294 Westbourne Gr, W11   229 1877   5-1B   ⁴⁷⁷

No one in search of culinary excitement would ever go anywhere near these cosy wine bar/restaurants, whose menus do not seem to have changed within living memory. They are convivial places, though, and have strong local followings at both their Chelsea branch (the nicer of the two, with a summer garden) and in Notting Hill. Deep-fried mushrooms (£3.90), chilli con carne (£5.50) and other similarly undemanding international fodder are the order of the day – every day. The house wine is £8. / 11 pm; no Amex.

Wolfe's   £ 15   ★
30 Gt Queen St, WC2   831 4442   3-1D   ⁴⁷⁸
25 Basil St, SW3   584 7217   4-1D   ⁴⁷⁹

It's for the reliable quality of their burgers (a half-pounder with chips is £7.25) that these two family restaurants are particularly well known, although other dishes, such as pastas and salads, are also available. The locations, behind Harrods and in east Covent Garden, help make them a particularly popular compromise choice for visitors with kids in tow. House wine is £8.95 a bottle. / 11.30 pm-midnight.

Wong Kei W1   £ 9   ★
41-43 Wardour St   437 8408   3-3A   ⁴⁸⁰

This vast, very inexpensive Cantonese restaurant in Chinatown is infamous for the intolerance of its staff. In fact, it's become so institutionalised now that it's widely regarded as part of the attraction of the place – so screw up your courage; don't object to sharing a table; don't delay over your ordering; don't hang around long after you've finished eating; and don't even think of trying to pay with anything other than cash. / 11.25 pm; no credit cards; no booking.

Wren at St James's SW1   £ 8   ★
197 Piccadilly   437 9419   2-2B   ⁴⁸¹

The café attached to this beautiful church offers an unusually central oasis, and the outside tables are particularly charming. The fare is all vegetarian – soup with bread (£2.35), chilli bean casserole with rice (£3.50), bake of the day (£4.25), salads (£2.65). Cakes (£1.40), mostly home-made, are a strength. No alcohol. / 7 pm; no credit cards; no smoking; no booking.

Wynkyn de Worde EC4 £ 9 –
482
1 St Brides Pas, Bride Ln   936 2554   8-3A

In the area around Fleet Street (which remains surprisingly thinly provided with tolerable eating places) this traditional wine bar (located near the 'wedding cake' church) is worth knowing about. You can either go for a sandwich (around £3), or one of the quite ambitious daily specials, such as seafood pancake or chicken risotto (for around a fiver). House wine is £7.80. The adjoining restaurant is significantly more expensive and not nearly such good value.
/ L only; closed Sat & Sun; no Switch.

Yum Yum N16 £ 15 A★
483
30 Stoke Newington Ch St   254 6751   1-1C

Stoke Newington isn't particularly renowned for its stylish restaurants, but this one offers a formula which combines a fair degree of chic with tasty, good value Thai cooking. There are set meals, for carnivores and for veggies, at around £13 – à la carte, you might get away with a fraction less. A bottle of Singha beer is £2.50. The place is quite large by local standards, but, even so, it's best to book. / 10.45 pm, Fri & Sat 11.45 pm.

Zamoyski NW3 £ 14 A★
484
85 Fleet Rd   794 4792   7-2A

This jolly, rustic Polish restaurant and wine bar near Belsize Park tube offers a warm welcome and good value. Either you can go à la carte, with dishes such as beetroot soup (£2) and stuffed cabbage (£5.50), or you could avail yourself of the '9 course meze' (which include soup and a pudding) for the same amount – an interesting, inexpensive light meal. House wine is £7.50. / 10.30 pm, Fri & Sat 11 pm; D only ex Sun, when open all day; no Amex & no Switch.

ZeNW3 NW3 £15* A★
485
83 Hampstead High St   794 7863   7-2A

This very stylish Chinese restaurant, with its glazed front and its internal waterfall, is a striking part of the Hampstead townscape. In the evening, it's out of our price range, but they do a £9.50 lunch menu of soup, followed by a 'banquet' of dim sum. House wine is £10. / 11.30 pm.

Indexes

Indexes

BYO
(Bring you own wine)

Central
Café Sofra – *W1, WC2*
Food for Thought
India Club
Neal's Yard Dining Rooms

West
Adam's Café
Bedlington Café
Blah! Blah! Blah!
Café Grove
Chelsea Bun Diner
Fat Boy's
El Gaucho
Kalamaras, Micro
Rôtisserie Jules
Topsy-Tasty

North
Ali Baba
Diwana Bhel-Poori House
Primrose Brasserie
Tsukushi
Upper St Fish Shop

South
Smokey Joe's

East
F Cooke & Sons
Lahore Kebab House
The Place Below

Children
(h – high or special chairs
m – children's menu
p – children's portions
e – weekend entertainments
o – other facilities)

Central
Ajimura *(h)*
Bahn Thai *(h)*
Boudin Blanc *(h)*
Café Pacifico *(hm)*
Chicago Pizza Pie Factory *(he)*
China Court *(h)*
Chuen Cheng Ku *(h)*
Claridges Causerie *(h)*
Como Lario *(h)*
Cranks – *W1, WC2 (h)*
Dragon Inn *(h)*
Ed's Easy Diner
Efes Kebab House – *W1 (p)*
Fortnum's Fountain *(h)*
Häagen-Dazs – *WC2 (h)*
Hard Rock Café *(h)*

Italian Kitchen *(mo)*
Kettners *(h)*
Marché Mövenpick *(p)*
Melati *(h)*
New World *(h)*
Pélican *(h)*
Pitcher & Piano – *WC2 (h)*
Pizza On The Park *(h)*
PizzaExpress – *W1, WC1, WC2 (h)*
Planet Hollywood *(hm)*
Porters *(hmo)*
Rock Garden *(hmo)*
Rock Island Diner *(hm)*
Smollensky's on the Strand
  (hmwo)
Tate Gallery *(h)*
Texas Embassy Cantina *(hm)*
TGI Friday's – *W1 (hme)*
Wagamama *(h)*
Wolfe's *(hm)*

West
L'Altro *(p)*
Basil St Hotel *(h)*
Benihana *(h)*
The Brackenbury *(h)*
Café Lazeez *(h)*
Café Météor *(h)*
Calzone *(mo)*
Ed's Easy Diner
Francofill *(h)*
Geale's *(h)*
Grill St Quentin *(hm)*
Jimmy Beez *(p)*
Joe's Brasserie *(m)*
Kalamaras, Micro *(p)*
Khan's *(h)*
Mackintosh's Brasserie *(h)*
Malabar *(h)*
Mandarin Kitchen *(h)*
Manzara *(h)*
Park Inn *(h)*
Phoenicia *(h)*
Pizza Chelsea *(hme)*
Pizza the Action *(h)*
PizzaExpress – *SW10, W11, W14,*
  W2, W4, W5, W8 (h)
PizzaExpress – *SW6 (ho)*
Royal China *(h)*
Shop *(hp)*
Sticky Fingers *(hmeo)*
Sushi Bar Gen *(h)*
Tandoori Nights *(hm)*
Texas Lone Star *(hm)*
Tootsies – *SW6, W11, W4 (hmo)*
Upstairs at
  the Basil Street *(hm)*
Wilson's *(h)*
Wine Gallery – *SW10, W11 (m)*
Wolfe's *(hm)*

Indexes

Ed's Easy Diner (Midnight, Fri & Sat
  1 am)
La Finca (1.30 am, Fri & Sat)
Greek Valley
House on Rosslyn Hill
Le Mercury (1 am)
PizzaExpress – N1, NW11, NW3
Sarcan
Tootsies (Fri & Sat)

South
Buona Sera
PizzaExpress – SE19, SW11, SW14,
  SW15, SW18, SW19
Primadonna
Tearoom des Artistes (Food
  available until late - licensed to 1am)
Tootsies (Fri & Sat)

East
Brick Lane Beigel Bake (24 hr)
Clifton (1 am)
Lahore Kebab House
Pizza Pomodoro – E1 (1 am)
The Shampan

No-smoking areas
(* completely no smoking)

Central
Ajimura
Café de Colombia*
Café Fish (Wine Bar)
Café Pacifico
Café Sofra – W1, WC2
Caravan Serai
Chicago Pizza Pie Factory
Cranks – W1, WC2*
The Criterion
Food for Thought*
Gopal's of Soho
Häagen-Dazs – WC2*
Hard Rock Café
Ikkyu – WC2
Mandeer*
Marché Mövenpick
Mildreds*
Ming
Museum St Café*
Neal's Yard Dining Rooms*
Oriel
Pizza On The Park
Planet Hollywood
Ristorante Italiano
Smollensky's on the Strand
Soho Soho
Tate Gallery
TGI Friday's – W1, WC2
Thai Pot
Tokyo Diner

Wagamama*
Wren at St James's*

West
Café Lazeez
Café Météor
Chutney Mary
Francofill
Häagen-Dazs – SW7, W2*
Joe's Brasserie
King's Road Café
Mackintosh's Brasserie
Mamta
Manzara
Mas Café
Nayab
Pizza Chelsea
S&P Patara
Stock Pot – SW3
Sushi Bar Gen
Sydney Street Café
Tiffin
Upstairs at
  the Basil Street

North
Anglo Asian Tandoori
Byron's
Casale Franco
Frederick's
Häagen-Dazs*
Marine Ices
Primrose Brasserie
Rani
Seashell

South
Eco
Gourmet Pizza Co. – SE1, SW19
Naked Turtle
The Stepping Stone
Twenty Trinity Gdns

East
Coates
Cranks*
Gourmet Pizza Co.
The Place Below*
Simpson's of Lloyds Avenue

Outside tables
(* particularly recommended)

Central
Bahn Thai
Bar Italia
Boudin Blanc*
Brahms*
Café Bohème
Café Sofra – W1*

Indexes

Modern British

ⓐ★★
Granita *(N1)*
Kensington Place *(W8)*
Launceston Place *(W8)*
Odette's *(NW1)*
The People's Palace *(SE1)*
Sonny's *(SW13)*
Walton's *(SW3)*
The Waterloo Fire
   Station *(SE1)*

★★
The Brackenbury *(W6)*
The Eagle *(EC1)*
Gilbert's *(SW7)*
Museum St Café *(WC1)*
Snows on the Green *(W6)*

ⓐ★
All Saints *(W11)*
Andrew Edmunds *(W1)*
Bar Central *(SW3, SE1)*
Byron's *(NW3)*
Café dell'Ugo *(SE1)*
Crown & Goose *(NW1)*
The Engineer *(NW1)*
English Garden *(SW3)*
English House *(SW3)*
The Fifth Floor *(SW1)*
Frocks *(E9)*
Lansdowne *(NW1)*
Lindsay House *(W1)*
Mars *(WC2)*
Mas Café *(W11)*
Quaglino's *(W1)*
Ransome's Dock *(SW11)*
Shillibeer's *(N7)*
The Stepping Stone *(SW8)*

★
Jimmy Beez *(W10)*
The Lexington *(W1)*
O'Keefe's *(W1)*
Odette's Wine Bar *(NW1)*
The Peasant *(EC1)*
Plummers *(WC2)*
Tattoo *(WC2)*
Wilson's *(W14)*

ⓐ
City Brasserie *(EC3)*
The Criterion *(W1)*
Tate Gallery *(SW1)*

–
Twenty Trinity Gdns *(SW9)*

Traditional British

ⓐ★★
Rules *(WC2)*
Simpson's of Cornhill *(EC3)*

ⓐ★
Maggie Jones's *(W8)*
Simpsons-in-the-Strand *(WC2)*

★
Fox & Anchor *(EC1)*
Porters *(WC2)*

ⓐ
Basil St Hotel *(SW3)*
Fortnum's Fountain *(W1)*
Olde Cheshire Cheese *(EC4)*
Windsor Castle *(W8)*

–
F Cooke & Sons *(E8)*

French

ⓐ★★
Brasserie St Quentin *(SW3)*
Frederick's *(N1)*
Mon Plaisir *(WC2)*
Shaw's *(SW7)*
Le Suquet *(SW3)*
Turner's *(SW3)*

★★
Lou Pescadou *(SW5)*

ⓐ★
Bleeding Heart *(EC1)*
La Bouchée *(SW7)*
Boudin Blanc *(W1)*
Brahms *(SW1)*
Café Bohème *(W1)*
Café de la Place *(SW11)*
Café Météor *(W6)*
La Cage Imaginaire *(NW3)*
Camden Brasserie *(NW1)*
Lobster Pot *(SE11)*
Mon Petit Plaisir *(W8)*
Le Palais du Jardin *(WC2)*
Pierre Victoire *(SW1, W1, SW10,
   W5, NW11, NW6, SW15)*
Soho Soho *(W1)*

★
Le Bouchon Bordelais *(SW11)*
Francofill *(SW7)*
Grill St Quentin *(SW3)*
Mustoe Bistro *(NW1)*
Le P'tit Normand *(SW18)*
La Rive Gauche *(SE1)*
Soulard *(N1)*

ⓐ
The Ark *(W8)*
Café Tabac *(SW15)*
Claridges Causerie *(W1)*

Cuisine indexes

Jigsaw *(W12)*
Le Mercury *(N1)*
Mustards Bistro à Vin *(EC1)*
Pélican *(WC2)*
Le Quai *(EC4)*
Thierry's *(SW3)*

–

Magno's Brasserie *(WC2)*
Rôtisserie Jules *(SW7)*

Belgian

Ⓐ★
Belgo Noord *(NW1)*

Italian

★★
L'Altro *(W11)*
The Red Pepper *(W9)*

Ⓐ★
Buona Sera *(SW11)*
Calzone *(W11, NW3)*
Casale Franco *(N1)*
De Cecco *(SW6)*
La Delizia *(SW3, SW5)*
Formula Veneta *(SW10)*
Marine Ices *(NW3)*
Osteria Basilico *(W11)*
Ristorante Italiano *(W1)*

★
Alba *(EC1)*
Arts Theatre Café *(WC2)*
Bersagliera *(SW3)*
Café Montpeliano *(SW3)*
Il Falconiere *(SW7)*
Italian Kitchen *(WC1)*
The Jam *(SW3)*
C Notarianni & Sons *(SW11)*
Ost. Antica Bologna *(SW11)*
Pizzeria Condotti *(W1)*
Pollo *(W1)*
Spago *(SW7)*

Ⓐ
A Tavola *(NW8)*
Como Lario *(SW1)*
La Fenice *(W11)*

–

Da Pierino *(SW7)*

Spanish

Ⓐ★★
Albero & Grana *(SW3)*

Ⓐ★
Bar Gansa *(NW1)*
Don Pepe *(NW8)*
La Finca *(N1, SE11)*

Galicia *(W10)*
Meson Don Felipe *(SE1)*
Meson Doña Ana *(W11)*
Rebato's *(SW8)*

★
Barcelona Tapas Bar *(E1)*
Los Remos *(W2)*

Ⓐ
Bar Madrid *(W1)*
Leadenhall Tapas Bar *(EC3)*
Rueda *(SW4)*

Greek

Ⓐ★★
Kalamaras, Mega *(W2)*
Kalamaras, Micro *(W2)*

★★
Greek Valley *(NW8)*

Ⓐ★
Lemonia *(NW1)*

★
Costa's Grill *(W8)*
Daphne *(NW1)*
Nontas *(NW1)*
Rodos *(WC2)*

–

Jimmy's *(W1)*
Wine & Kebab *(SW10)*

Middle Eastern

Ⓐ★★
Café Sofra *(W1, WC2)*
Efes Kebab House *(W1)*

Ⓐ★
Maroush *(SW3)*
Maroush *(W2)*
Sofra *(W1, WC2)*

★
Ali Baba *(NW1)*
Gaby's *(WC2)*
Manzara *(W11)*
Phoenicia *(W8)*
Ranoush *(W1)*
Sarcan *(N1)*
Topkapi *(W1)*

German

★
Cosmo *(NW3)*
Prost *(W11)*

Scandinavian

Ⓐ
Claridges Causerie *(W1)*

110

–
Garbo's *(WI)*

Hungarian

★
Prost *(WII)*

Czech

★
Czech Club *(NW6)*

Polish

Ⓐ★
Zamoyski *(NW3)*

Ⓐ
Daquise *(SW7)*
Ognisko Polskie *(SW7)*
Primrose Brasserie *(NWI)*

Russian

Ⓐ
Primrose Brasserie *(NWI)*

Kosher

★
Nautilus *(NW6)*

–
Bloom's *(EI)*

International

Ⓐ★
606 Club *(SW10)*
Café Delancey *(NWI)*
Coopers Arms *(SW3)*
Cork & Bottle *(WC2)*
Dôme *(WC2, SW3, W8, NI, NW3, SW19)*
Front Page *(SW3)*
Joe's Wine Bar *(SWII)*
Mackintosh's Brasserie *(W4)*
Mongolian Barbecue *(SW6, SW7, W5, SWII, SW15, SW19)*
Naked Turtle *(SW14)*
Pitcher & Piano *(WI, WC2, SW10, SW6, W4)*
The Ship *(SW18)*
Stock Pot *(SWI, WI, SW3)*
Wine Gallery *(SW10, WII)*
Wolfe's *(WC2, SW3)*

★
Chelsea Bun Diner *(SW10)*
Chelsea Kitchen *(SW3)*
Cosmo *(NW3)*
Marché Mövenpick *(WI)*

Simpson's of Lloyds
    Avenue *(EC3)*
Upstairs at
    the Basil Street *(SW3)*

Ⓐ
Archduke Wine Bar *(SEI)*
Banners *(N8)*
Batt. Barge Bistro *(SW8)*
Café Grove *(WII)*
Caffe Graffiti *(NW3)*
The Depot *(SW14)*
Dove *(W6)*
Ebury Street Wine Bar *(SWI)*
Foxtrot Oscar *(SW3)*
Gordon's Wine Bar *(WC2)*
Hoults *(SW17)*
House on Rosslyn Hill *(NW3)*
Joe's Brasserie *(SW6)*
Oriel *(SWI)*
Rock Garden *(WC2)*
Ruby in the Dust *(NI, NWI, SWII)*
The Scarsdale *(W8)*
Shampers *(WI)*
South Bank Brasserie *(SEI)*
Sydney Street Café *(SW3)*
Windsor Castle *(W8)*

–
Granary *(WI)*
Star Café *(WI)*
Up All Night *(SW10)*
Wynkyn de Worde *(EC4)*

Fish & seafood

Ⓐ★★
Le Suquet *(SW3)*

★★
L'Altro *(WII)*
Lou Pescadou *(SW5)*

Ⓐ★
Belgo Noord *(NWI)*
Bibendum Oyster Bar *(SW3)*
Lobster Pot *(SEII)*
Quaglino's *(WI)*

★
Café Fish (Wine Bar) *(SWI)*

–
F Cooke & Sons *(E8)*

Fish & chips

★★
Geale's *(W8)*
Toff's *(N10)*

Ⓐ★
Upper St Fish Shop *(NI)*

Cuisine indexes

★
Brady's *(SW18)*
Nautilus *(NW6)*
Seashell *(NW1)*

South American

★★
Fina Estampa *(SE1)*

Ⓐ★
El Gaucho *(SW3)*

★
Paulo's *(W6)*

Ⓐ
Bar Madrid *(W1)*

Mexican/TexMex

Ⓐ★
Dixie's Bar & Grill *(SW11)*

Ⓐ
Café Pacifico *(WC2)*
Down Mexico Way *(W1)*
Texas Embassy Cantina *(WC2)*

American

Ⓐ★
TGI Friday's *(W1, WC2)*

Ⓐ
Hard Rock Café *(W1)*
Rock Island Diner *(W1)*
Smollensky's on the
    Strand *(WC2)*
Sticky Fingers *(W8)*

Steaks & grills

Ⓐ★★
Simpson's of Cornhill *(EC3)*

Ⓐ★
Camden Brasserie *(NW1)*
El Gaucho *(SW3)*
Quaglino's *(W1)*
Rôtisserie *(W12)*
Soho Soho *(W1)*

★
Fox & Anchor *(EC1)*

Ⓐ
Kettners *(W1)*
Smollensky's on the
    Strand *(WC2)*

–
Hope & Sir Loin *(EC1)*

Burgers, etc

Ⓐ★
Ed's Easy Diner *(W1, SW3, NW3)*
Tootsies *(SW6, W11, W4, SW13,
    SW19)*
Wolfe's *(WC2, SW3)*

Ⓐ
Foxtrot Oscar *(SW3)*
Hard Rock Café *(W1)*
Joe's Brasserie *(SW6)*
Planet Hollywood *(W1)*
Rock Garden *(WC2)*
Rock Island Diner *(W1)*
Ruby in the Dust *(N1, NW1,
    SW11)*
Sticky Fingers *(W8)*
Texas Lone Star *(SW7)*

Pizza

Ⓐ★★
Eco *(SW4)*

★★
The Red Pepper *(W9)*

Ⓐ★
Buona Sera *(SW11)*
Calzone *(W11, NW3)*
Casale Franco *(N1)*
La Delizia *(SW3, SW5)*
Gourmet Pizza Co. *(SE1, SW19,
    E14)*
Marine Ices *(NW3)*
Pizza On The Park *(SW1)*
Pizza Pomodoro *(SW3, E1, EC1)*
Pizza the Action *(SW6)*
PizzaExpress *(W1, WC1, WC2,
    SW10, SW6, W11, W14, W2, W4, W5,
    W8, N1, NW11, NW3, SE1, SE19,
    SW11, SW14, SW15, SW18, SW19)*
Pizzeria Castello *(SE1)*

★
Coates *(EC2)*
C Notarianni & Sons *(SW11)*
Primadonna *(SW11)*
Spago *(SW7)*

Ⓐ
Da Mario *(SW7)*
Kettners *(W1)*
Pucci Pizza *(SW3)*

–
Chicago Pizza Pie
    Factory *(W1)*
Pizza Chelsea *(SW3)*

Afternoon tea

Ⓐ
Basil St Hotel *(SW3)*

The Criterion *(W1)*
Daquise *(SW7)*
Fortnum's Fountain *(W1)*
Hyde Park Hotel
  Park Room *(SW1)*
Ognisko Polskie *(SW7)*
Orangery *(W8)*
Waldorf Hotel *(WC2)*

Snacks

𝔸★★
Lisboa Patisserie *(W10)*
Pret A Manger *(SW1, W1, WC2, SW3, N1, EC2, EC4)*
★★
Brick Lane Beigel Bake *(E1)*
𝔸★
Café de Colombia *(W1)*
Fileric *(SW7, SW8)*
King's Road Café *(SW3)*
Pâtisserie Valerie at
  Sagne *(W1, SW3)*
★
Café Montpeliano *(SW3)*
Manzara *(W11)*
𝔸
Bar Italia *(W1)*
Café Grove *(W11)*
Maison Bertaux *(W1)*
Shop *(SW3)*
Troubadour *(SW5)*

Ice cream

𝔸★
Häagen-Dazs *(WC2, SW7, W2, NW3)*
Marine Ices *(NW3)*
★
C Notarianni & Sons *(SW11)*
𝔸
Fortnum's Fountain *(W1)*

Afro-Caribbean

★
Smokey Joe's *(SW18)*
–
Calabash *(WC2)*

Tunisian

𝔸★★
Adam's Café *(W12)*
★★
Laurent *(NW2)*

Afghani

𝔸★
Caravan Serai *(W1)*

Indian

★★
Diwana Bhel-Poori
  House *(NW1)*
Kastoori *(SW17)*
Lahore Kebab House *(E1)*
Namaste *(E1)*
Rani *(N3)*
𝔸★
Café Lazeez *(SW7)*
Gopal's in the City *(EC2)*
Mandeer *(W1)*
Planet Poppadom *(SW3)*
Tandoori Lane *(SW6)*
★
Chutney Mary *(SW10)*
Chutneys *(NW1)*
Clifton *(E1)*
Geeta *(NW6)*
Gopal's of Soho *(W1)*
Haandi *(NW1)*
Karahi *(NW6)*
Khyber Pass *(SW7)*
Lalbag *(W11)*
Ma Goa *(SW15)*
Mamta *(SW6)*
Nayab *(SW6)*
The Shampan *(E1)*
Shree Krishna *(SW17)*
Standard Tandoori *(W2)*
Tandoori Nights *(W6)*
Tiffin *(SW6)*
Vijay *(NW6)*
𝔸
Anglo Asian Tandoori *(N16)*
Khan's of Kensington *(SW7)*
Khan's *(W2)*
Malabar *(W8)*
Nizam *(SW5)*
–
India Club *(WC2)*
Veeraswamy *(W1)*

Thai

𝔸★★
Churchill *(W8)*
★★
Bahn Thai *(W1)*
Bedlington Café *(W4)*
Sri Siam *(W1)*
Thailand *(SE14)*
Topsy-Tasty *(W4)*

Cuisine indexes

⚊★
Ben's Thai *(W9)*
Fat Boy's *(W4)*
Sash *(SW6)*
Thai Pot *(WC2)*
Yum Yum *(N16)*

★
Bangkok *(SW7)*
Blue Jade *(SW1)*
Chaba *(SW10)*
Chiang Mai *(W1)*
Krungtap *(SW10)*
Latymers *(W6)*
S&P Patara *(SW3)*
S&P *(SW3)*
Thai Kitchen *(W2)*
Tuk Tuk *(N1)*

⚊
Dove *(W6)*

Malaysian

★
Melati *(W1)*
Singapore Garden *(NW6)*
⚊
Jim Thompson's *(SW6)*

Vietnamese

⚊
Mekong *(SW1)*

Chinese

⚊★★
Poons *(WC2)*
Royal China *(W2, SW15)*
★★
Fung Shing *(WC2)*
Harbour City *(W1)*
Mayflower *(W1)*
Mr Kong *(WC2)*
Poons, Lisle Street *(WC2)*
⚊★
Ming *(W1)*
West Zenders *(WC2)*
ZeNW3 *(NW3)*

★
China Court *(W1)*
Dragon Inn *(W1)*
Hong Kong *(WC2)*
Mandarin Kitchen *(W2)*
Park Inn *(W2)*
Poons in the City *(EC3)*
Wong Kei *(W1)*

–
Chuen Cheng Ku *(W1)*

New World *(W1)*

Chinese

★
Singapore Garden *(NW6)*
⚊
Mekong *(SW1)*

Dim sum

⚊★★
Royal China *(W2, SW15)*
★★
Harbour City *(W1)*
⚊★
Ming *(W1)*
★
China Court *(W1)*
Dragon Inn *(W1)*
Hong Kong *(WC2)*

–
Chuen Cheng Ku *(W1)*
New World *(W1)*

Korean

★
Bu San *(N7)*

Japanese

⚊★★
Benihana *(W1, SW3, NW3)*
Ikkyu *(W1, WC2)*
Wagamama *(WC1)*
★★
Ajimura *(WC2)*
Inaho *(W2)*
Moshi Moshi Sushi *(EC2)*
⚊★
Noto *(EC2, EC4)*

★
Aykoku-Kaku *(EC4)*
Benkei *(SE1)*
Bu San *(N7)*
Hamine *(W1)*
Sumos *(W6)*
Sushi Bar Gen *(SW6)*
Tokyo Diner *(WC2)*
Tsukushi *(NW1)*

–
Imari *(WC1)*
Jin Kichi *(NW3)*

Area overviews

CENTRAL

Soho & Covent Garden (and Bloomsbury)
(Parts of W1, all WC1 and WC2)

£15+	Museum St Café	Modern British	(★★)
	Andrew Edmunds	"	𝔸★
	Lindsay House	"	(𝔸★)
	Mars	"	𝔸★
	Plummers	"	★
	Tattoo	"	★
	The Criterion	"	𝔸
	Rules	Traditional British	(𝔸★★)
	Simpsons-in-the-Strand	"	(𝔸★)
	Porters	"	★
	Café Bohème	French	𝔸★
	Le Palais du Jardin	"	𝔸★
	Soho Soho	"	𝔸★
	Pélican	"	𝔸
	Magno's Brasserie	"	–
	Pierre Victoire	"	–
	Arts Theatre Café	Italian	★
	Italian Kitchen	"	★
	Sofra	Middle Eastern	𝔸★
	Wolfe's	International	★
	Café Pacifico	Mexican/TexMex	𝔸
	Texas Embassy Cantina	"	𝔸
	Smollensky's on the Strand	American	𝔸
	TGI Friday's	"	𝔸
	Planet Hollywood	Burgers, etc	𝔸
	Gopal's of Soho	Indian	★
	Bahn Thai	Thai	★★
	Sri Siam	"	★★
	Thai Pot	"	𝔸★
	Chiang Mai	"	★
	Melati	Malaysian	★
	Fung Shing	Chinese	★★
	Mayflower	"	★★
	Ming	"	𝔸★
	West Zenders	"	𝔸★
	Hong Kong	"	★
	Ajimura	Japanese	(★★)
	Ikkyu	"	★★
	Imari	"	–
£10+	The Lexington	Modern British	★
	Mon Plaisir	French	(𝔸★★)
	Rodos	Greek	★
	Jimmy's	"	–
	Cork & Bottle	International	𝔸★

	Dôme	"	𝔸★
	Pitcher & Piano	"	𝔸★
	Marché Mövenpick	"	★
	Gordon's Wine Bar	"	𝔸
	Rock Garden	"	𝔸
	Shampers	"	𝔸
	Cranks	*Vegetarian*	★
	Mildreds	"	★
	Rock Island Diner	*American*	𝔸
	PizzaExpress	*Pizza*	𝔸★
	Kettners	"	𝔸
	Waldorf Hotel	*Afternoon tea*	(𝔸)
	Calabash	*Afro-Caribbean*	–
	India Club	*Indian*	–
	Poons	*Chinese*	𝔸★★
	Harbour City	"	★★
	Mr Kong	"	★★
	Poons, Lisle Street	"	★★
	China Court	"	★
	Dragon Inn	"	★
	Chuen Cheng Ku	"	–
	New World	"	–
	Wagamama	*Japanese*	𝔸★★
	Tokyo Diner	"	★
£5+	Pollo	*Italian*	★
	Café Sofra	*Middle Eastern*	𝔸★★
	Gaby's	"	★
	Stock Pot	*International*	★
	Food for Thought	*Vegetarian*	★★
	Neal's Yard Dining Rooms	"	★
	Ed's Easy Diner	*Burgers, etc*	
	Pret A Manger	*Snacks*	★★
	Pâtisserie Valerie	"	𝔸★
	Wong Kei	*Chinese*	★
	Hamine	*Japanese*	★
£1+	Star Café	*International*	–
	Bar Italia	*Snacks*	𝔸
	Maison Bertaux	"	𝔸
	Häagen-Dazs	*Ice cream*	–

Mayfair & St James's
(Parts of W1 and SW1)

£15+	Quaglino's	*Modern British*	(𝔸★)
	O'Keefe's	"	★
	Fortnum's Fountain	*Traditional British*	𝔸
	Boudin Blanc	*French*	𝔸★
	Claridges Causerie	"	(𝔸)
	Pierre Victoire	"	–

Area lists

	Ristorante Italiano	*Italian*	𝔸★
	Sofra	*Middle Eastern*	𝔸★
	Down Mexico Way	*Mexican/TexMex*	𝔸
	Veeraswamy	*Indian*	(–)
£10+	Pizzeria Condotti	*Italian*	★
	Granary	*International*	–
	Café Fish (Wine Bar)	*Fish & seafood*	★
	Hard Rock Café	*Burgers, etc*	𝔸
	Chicago Pizza Pie Factory	*Pizza*	–
	Café de Colombia Museum of Mankind	*Snacks*	𝔸★
	Benihana	*Japanese*	(𝔸★★)
£5+	Café Sofra	*Middle Eastern*	𝔸★★
	Stock Pot	*International*	★
	Wren at St James's	*Vegetarian*	★
	Pret A Manger	*Snacks*	★★

North of Oxford Street
(Part of W1)

£15+	Garbo's	*Scandinavian*	–
	Caravan Serai	*Afghani*	𝔸★
	Ikkyu	*Japanese*	★★
£10+	Bar Madrid	*Spanish*	𝔸
	Efes Kebab House	*Middle Eastern*	𝔸★★
	Topkapi	*"*	★
	Cranks	*Vegetarian*	★
	Mandeer	*Indian*	𝔸★
£5+	Ranoush	*Middle Eastern*	★
	Stock Pot	*International*	★
	Pret A Manger	*Snacks*	★★
	Pâtisserie Valerie at Sagne	*"*	𝔸★

Belgravia, Victoria, Pimlico
(SW1, except St James's)

£20+	The Fifth Floor	*Modern British*	𝔸★
£15+	Tate Gallery	*Modern British*	𝔸
	Como Lario	*Italian*	𝔸
	Ebury Street Wine Bar	*International*	𝔸
	Oriel	*"*	𝔸
	Hyde Park Hotel Park Room	*Afternoon tea*	(𝔸)
	Blue Jade	*Thai*	★

	Mekong	*Vietnamese*	𝔸
£10+	Pizza On The Park	*Pizza*	𝔸★
£5+	Brahms	*French*	𝔸★
	Pret A Manger	*Snacks*	★★

WEST

Chelsea, South Kensington, Kensington, Earl's Court, Fulham (SW3, SW5, SW6, SW7, SW10 & W8)

£20+	Walton's	*Modern British*	(𝔸★★)
	English Garden	"	(𝔸★)
	English House	"	(𝔸★)
	Shaw's	*French*	(𝔸★★)
£15+	Kensington Place	*Modern British*	(𝔸★★)
	Launceston Place	"	(𝔸★★)
	Gilbert's	"	(★★)
	Bar Central	"	𝔸★
	Maggie Jones's	*Traditional British*	(𝔸★)
	Basil St Hotel	"	(𝔸)
	Brasserie St Quentin	*French*	(𝔸★★)
	Le Suquet	"	(𝔸★★)
	Turner's	"	(𝔸★★)
	Lou Pescadou	"	(★★)
	La Bouchée	"	𝔸★
	Mon Petit Plaisir	"	(𝔸★)
	Emile's	"	★
	The Ark	"	𝔸
	Thierry's	"	(𝔸)
	Pierre Victoire	"	–
	De Cecco	*Italian*	𝔸★
	Formula Veneta	"	𝔸★
	Il Falconiere	"	★
	Albero & Grana	*Spanish*	𝔸★★
	606 Club	*International*	𝔸★
	Foxtrot Oscar	"	𝔸
	Joe's Brasserie	"	𝔸
	Wolfe's	"	★
	Bibendum Oyster Bar	*Fish & seafood*	𝔸★
	Da Mario	*Pizza*	𝔸
	Pizza Pomodoro	"	𝔸
	Pucci Pizza	"	𝔸
	Café Lazeez	*Indian*	𝔸★
	Tandoori Lane	"	𝔸★
	Chutney Mary	"	(★)
	Nayab	"	★
	Khan's of Kensington	"	𝔸

	Nizam	"	𝔸
	Chaba	*Thai*	★
	S&P	"	★
	S&P Patara	"	★
	Jim Thompson's	*Malaysian*	𝔸
	Sushi Bar Gen	*Japanese*	★
£10+	Francofill	*French*	★
	Grill St Quentin	"	(★)
	Bersagliera	*Italian*	★
	Café Montpeliano	"	★
	The Jam	"	★
	Spago	"	★
	Da Pierino	"	–
	Wine & Kebab	*Greek*	–
	Maroush	*Middle Eastern*	𝔸★
	Phoenicia	"	(★)
	Daquise	*Polish*	𝔸
	Ognisko Polskie	"	𝔸
	Coopers Arms	*International*	𝔸★
	Dôme	"	𝔸★
	Front Page	"	𝔸★
	Pitcher & Piano	"	𝔸★
	Upstairs at the Basil Street	"	★
	The Scarsdale	"	𝔸
	Sydney Street Café	"	𝔸
	Windsor Castle	"	𝔸
	Wine Gallery	"	𝔸
	Mongolian Barbecue	"	–
	Up All Night	"	–
	Geale's	*Fish & chips*	★★
	El Gaucho	*South American*	𝔸★
	Sticky Fingers	*American*	𝔸
	Tootsies	*Burgers, etc*	★
	Texas Lone Star	"	𝔸
	La Delizia	*Pizza*	𝔸★
	Pizza the Action	"	𝔸★
	PizzaExpress	"	𝔸★
	Pizza Chelsea	"	–
	Orangery	*Afternoon tea*	𝔸
	King's Road Café	*Snacks*	𝔸★
	Shop	"	𝔸
	Planet Poppadom	*Indian*	𝔸★
	Khyber Pass	"	★
	Mamta	"	★
	Tiffin	"	★
	Malabar	"	𝔸
	Sash	*Thai*	𝔸★
	Bangkok	"	★
	Krungtap	"	★
	Benihana	*Japanese*	(𝔸★★)

£5+	Rôtisserie Jules	*French*	–
	Costa's Grill	*Greek*	★
	Chelsea Bun Diner	*International*	★
	Chelsea Kitchen	*"*	★
	Stock Pot	*"*	★
	Ed's Easy Diner	*Burgers, etc*	–
	Pret A Manger	*Snacks*	★★
	Pâtisserie Valerie	*"*	🄰★
	Troubadour	*"*	🄰
	Churchill	*Thai*	🄰★★
£1+	Fileric	*Snacks*	★
	Häagen-Dazs	*Ice cream*	–

Notting Hill, Holland Park, Bayswater, North Kensington & Maida Vale (W2, W9, W10, W11)

£15+	All Saints	*Modern British*	🄰★
	Mas Café	*"*	(🄰★)
	Jimmy Beez	*"*	★
	Osteria Basilico	*Italian*	🄰★
	La Fenice	*"*	🄰
	Galicia	*Spanish*	🄰★
	Kalamaras, Mega	*Greek*	🄰★★
	Thai Kitchen	*Thai*	★
	Mandarin Kitchen	*Chinese*	★
	Park Inn	*"*	★
	Inaho	*Japanese*	★★
£10+	L'Altro	*Italian*	(★★)
	The Red Pepper	*"*	★★
	Calzone	*"*	🄰★
	Meson Doña Ana	*Spanish*	🄰★
	Los Remos	*"*	★
	Kalamaras, Micro	*Greek*	🄰★★
	Maroush	*Middle Eastern*	🄰★
	Manzara	*"*	★
	Prost	*German*	★
	Café Grove	*International*	🄰
	Wine Gallery	*"*	🄰
	Tootsies	*Burgers, etc*	★
	PizzaExpress	*Pizza*	🄰★
	Lalbag	*Indian*	★
	Standard Tandoori	*"*	★
	Khan's	*"*	🄰
	Ben's Thai	*Thai*	🄰★
	Royal China	*Chinese*	(🄰★★)
£5+	Street Hawker	*Malaysian*	(★)

Area lists

| £1+ | Lisboa Patisserie | *Snacks* | 𝔸★★ |
| | Häagen-Dazs | *Ice cream* | – |

Hammersmith, Shepherd's Bush Chiswick & Olympia (W4, W5, W6, W12, W14)

£15+	The Brackenbury	*Modern British*	★★
	Snows on the Green	"	(★★)
	Wilson's	"	★
	Pierre Victoire	*French*	–
	Mackintosh's Brasserie	*International*	𝔸★
	Blah! Blah! Blah!	*Vegetarian*	★
	Rôtisserie	*Steaks & grills*	𝔸★

£10+	Café Météor	*French*	𝔸★
	Jigsaw	"	𝔸
	Pitcher & Piano	*International*	𝔸★
	Mongolian Barbecue	"	–
	The Gate	*Vegetarian*	𝔸★
	Paulo's	*South American*	★
	Tootsies	*Burgers, etc*	★
	PizzaExpress	*Pizza*	𝔸★
	Adam's Café	*Tunisian*	𝔸★★
	Tandoori Nights	*Indian*	★
	Bedlington Café	*Thai*	★★
	Topsy-Tasty	"	★★
	Fat Boy's	"	𝔸★
	Sumos	*Japanese*	★

| £5+ | Dove | *International* | 𝔸 |
| | Latymers | *Thai* | ★ |

NORTH

Hampstead, West Hampstead, St John's Wood, Regent's Park, Kilburn & Camden Town (NW postcodes)

£15+	Odette's	*Modern British*	(𝔸★★)
	Lansdowne	"	𝔸★
	Odette's Wine Bar	"	★
	La Cage Imaginaire	*French*	(𝔸★)
	Camden Brasserie	"	𝔸★
	Pierre Victoire	"	–
	Belgo Noord	*Belgian*	𝔸★
	A Tavola	*Italian*	𝔸
	Lemonia	*Greek*	𝔸★
	Café Delancey	*International*	𝔸★

	Cosmo	"	★
	Caffe Graffiti	"	Ⓐ
	House on Rosslyn Hill	"	Ⓐ
	Seashell	Fish & chips	★
	Laurent	Tunisian	★★
	Singapore Garden	Malaysian	★
	ZeNW3	Chinese	(Ⓐ★)
£10+	Byron's	Modern British	(Ⓐ★)
	Crown & Goose	"	Ⓐ★
	The Engineer	"	Ⓐ★
	Mustoe Bistro	French	★
	Calzone	Italian	Ⓐ★
	Marine Ices	"	Ⓐ★
	Bar Gansa	Spanish	Ⓐ★
	Don Pepe	"	Ⓐ★
	Greek Valley	Greek	★★
	Daphne	"	★
	Nontas	"	★
	Ali Baba	Middle Eastern	★
	Czech Club	Czech	★
	Zamoyski	Polish	Ⓐ★
	Primrose Brasserie	Russian	Ⓐ
	Dôme	International	Ⓐ★
	Ruby in the Dust	"	Ⓐ
	Nautilus	Fish & chips	★
	PizzaExpress	Pizza	Ⓐ★
	Geeta	Indian	★
	Haandi	"	★
	Karahi	"	★
	Vijay	"	★
	Benihana	Japanese	(Ⓐ★★)
	Tsukushi	"	★
	Jin Kichi	"	–
£5+	Ed's Easy Diner	Burgers, etc	–
	Diwana B.-Poori Hs	Indian	★★
	Chutneys	"	★
£1+	Häagen-Dazs	Ice cream	–

Islington, Highgate, Crouch End, Stoke Newington, Finsbury Park, Muswell Hill & Finchley (N postcodes)

£15+	Granita	Modern British	(Ⓐ★★)
	Shillibeer's	"	Ⓐ★
	Frederick's	French	(Ⓐ★★)
	Soulard	"	★
	Casale Franco	Italian	Ⓐ★

	Rani	*Indian*	★★
	Yum Yum	*Thai*	🅰★
	Bu San	*Korean*	★
£10+	Le Mercury	*French*	🅰
	La Finca	*Spanish*	🅰
	Sarcan	*Middle Eastern*	★
	Dôme	*International*	🅰★
	Banners	*"*	🅰
	Ruby in the Dust	*"*	🅰
	Toff's	*Fish & chips*	★★
	Upper St Fish Shop	*"*	🅰★
	PizzaExpress	*Pizza*	🅰★
	Anglo Asian Tandoori	*Indian*	🅰
	Tuk Tuk	*Thai*	★
£5+	Pret A Manger	*Snacks*	★★

SOUTH

South Bank
(SE1)

£15+	The People's Palace	*Modern British*	🅰★★
	The Waterloo Fire Station	*"*	🅰★★
	Bar Central	*"*	🅰★
	La Rive Gauche	*French*	★
	South Bank Brasserie	*International*	🅰
	Fina Estampa	*South American*	★★
£10+	Café dell'Ugo	*Modern British*	🅰★
	Meson Don Felipe	*Spanish*	🅰★
	Archduke Wine Bar	*International*	🅰
	PizzaExpress	*Pizza*	🅰★
	Pizzeria Castello	*"*	🅰★
	Gourmet Pizza Co.	*"*	★
	Benkei	*Japanese*	★

Battersea, Clapham, Wandsworth, Barnes, Putney, Brixton, Lewisham
(All postcodes south of the river except SE1)

£20+	Lobster Pot	*Fish & seafood*	(🅰★)
£15+	Sonny's	*Modern British*	🅰★★
	Ransome's Dock	*"*	(🅰★)
	The Stepping Stone	*"*	🅰★
	Twenty Trinity Gdns	*"*	–
	Café de la Place	*French*	🅰★

	Le Bouchon Bordelais	"	★
	Emile's	"	★
	Le P'tit Normand	"	★
	Pierre Victoire	"	–
	Ost. Antica Bologna	*Italian*	★
	Naked Turtle	*International*	𝔸★
	The Depot	"	𝔸
	Hoults	"	𝔸
	C Notarianni & Sons	*Pizza*	★
	Thailand	*Thai*	★★
£10+	Café Tabac	*French*	𝔸
	Buona Sera	*Italian*	𝔸★
	Rebato's	*Spanish*	𝔸★
	La Finca	"	𝔸
	Rueda	"	𝔸
	Dôme	*International*	𝔸★
	Joe's Wine Bar	"	𝔸★
	The Ship	"	𝔸★
	Batt. Barge Bistro	"	𝔸
	Ruby in the Dust	"	𝔸
	Mongolian Barbecue	"	–
	Tearoom des Artistes	*Vegetarian*	★
	Brady's	*Fish & chips*	★
	Dixie's Bar & Grill	*Mexican/TexMex*	𝔸★
	Tootsies	*Burgers, etc*	★
	Eco	*Pizza*	𝔸★★
	PizzaExpress	"	𝔸★
	Gourmet Pizza Co.	"	★
	Primadonna	"	★
	Kastoori	*Indian*	★★
	Ma Goa	"	★
	Shree Krishna	"	★
	Royal China	*Chinese*	𝔸★★
£5+	Smokey Joe's	*Afro-Caribbean*	★
£1+	Fileric	*Snacks*	★

EAST

Smithfield, Farringdon (EC1)

£15+	The Peasant	*Modern British*	★
	Bleeding Heart	*French*	(𝔸★)
	Mustards Bistro à Vin	"	𝔸
	Alba	*Italian*	★
	Pizza Pomodoro	*Pizza*	𝔸
£10+	The Eagle	*Modern British*	★★

Area lists

Fox & Anchor	*Traditional British*	(★)
Carnevale	*Vegetarian*	★
Cranks	"	★
Hope & Sir Loin	*Steaks & grills*	(–)

The City and East End
(All E and EC postcodes, except EC1)

£15+	Frocks	*Modern British*	𝔸★
	City Brasserie	"	(𝔸)
	Bloom's	*Kosher*	–
	Pizza Pomodoro	*Pizza*	𝔸
	Namaste	*Indian*	★★
	Gopal's in the City	"	𝔸★
	Aykoku-Kaku	*Japanese*	★
£10+	Simpson's of Cornhill	*Traditional British*	𝔸★★
	Ye Olde Chesh. Cheese	"	𝔸
	Le Quai	*French*	𝔸
	Barcelona Tapas Bar	*Spanish*	★
	Leadenhall Tapas Bar	"	𝔸
	Simpson's of Lloyds Avenue	*International*	★
	Futures	*Vegetarian*	★★
	The Place Below	"	★★
	Coates	*Pizza*	★
	Gourmet Pizza Co.	"	★
	Clifton	*Indian*	★
	The Shampan	"	★
	Poons in the City	*Chinese*	★
	Noto	*Japanese*	★
£5+	Wynkyn de Worde	*International*	–
	F Cooke & Sons	*Fish & seafood*	
	Pret A Manger	*Snacks*	★★
	Lahore Kebab House	*Indian*	★★
	Moshi Moshi Sushi	*Japanese*	★★
£1+	Brick Lane Beigel Bake	*Snacks*	★★

Maps

Map 1 – Overview

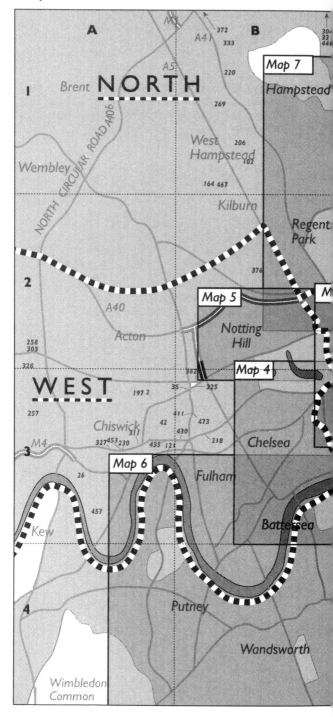

A   372   B
333

A41

A5   220

I   Brent   **NORTH**

Map 7

Hampstead

269

West   206
Hampstead   102

Wembley

164 467

Kilburn

Regent Park

NORTH CIRCULAR ROAD A406

376

2

Map 5

A40

Notting Hill

258
303

Acton

328

Map 4

W E S T   197 2   35   325

257

411
42   473

Chiswick   430

327 453 230   435 121   218   *Chelsea*

M4

3   26

Map 6

Fulham

457

Kew

Battersea

4

Putney

Wandsworth

Wimbledon Common

Map 1 – Overview

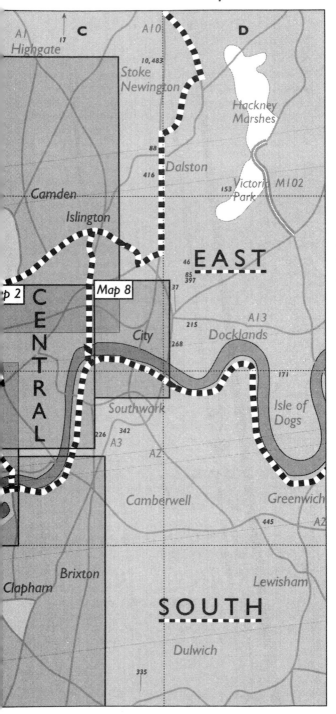

Map 2 – Central

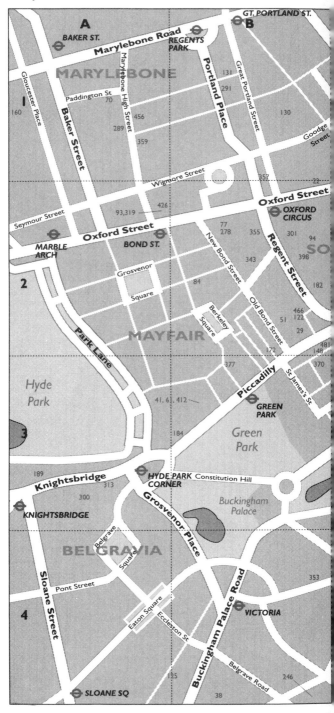

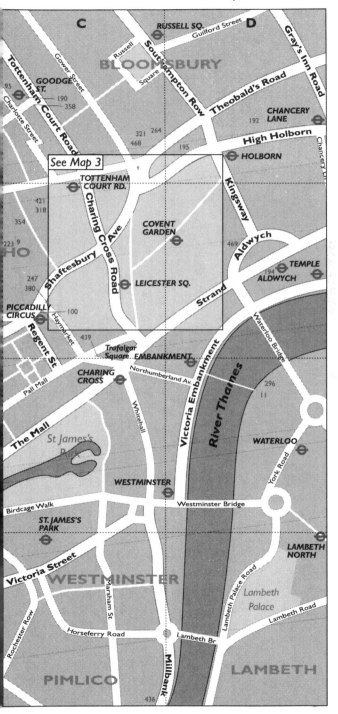

Map 2 – Central

Map 3 – West End (blow-up)

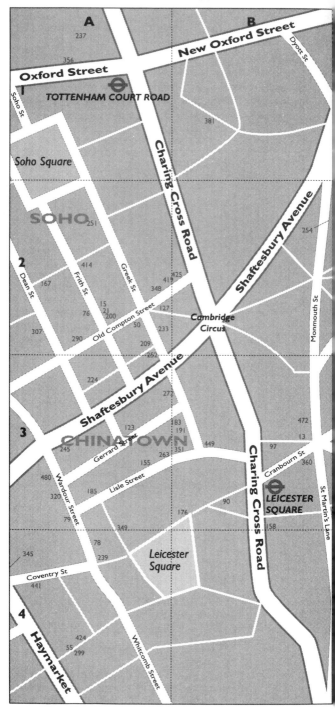

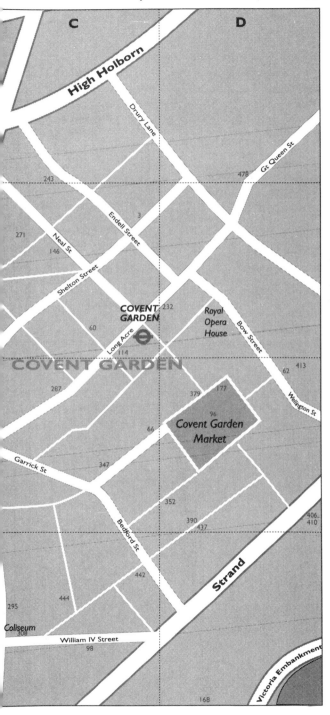

Map 3 – West End (blow-up)

Map 4 – West (SW postcodes)

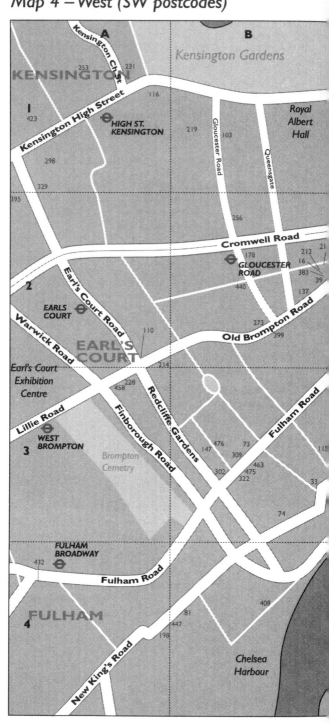

A

B

Kensington Ch.

Kensington Gardens

253   231

KENSINGTON

116

I
423

Kensington High Street

HIGH ST.
KENSINGTON

219

103

Gloucester Road

*Royal
Albert
Hall*

298

Queensgate

329

395

256

Cromwell Road

178

212   21

16

**GLOUCESTER
ROAD**

383   39

Earl's Court Road

440

137

2

EARLS
COURT

273

Old Brompton Road

399

Warwick Road

110

**EARL'S
COURT**

214

*Earl's Court
Exhibition
Centre*

458   228

Redcliffe Gardens

Finborough Road

Fulham Road

Lillie Road

147   476   73
309

115

3

WEST
BROMPTON

*Brompton
Cemetery*

302   475
322   463

33

74

**FULHAM
BROADWAY**

432

Fulham Road

408

FULHAM

81

4

447

198

New King's Road

*Chelsea
Harbour*

Map 4 – West (SW postcodes)

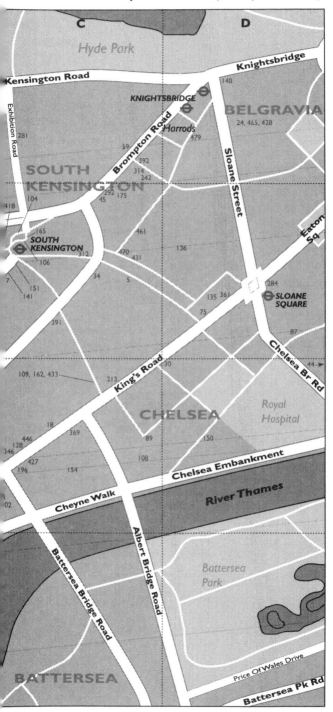

C   D

Hyde Park

Knightsbridge

Kensington Road

KNIGHTSBRIDGE

BELGRAVIA

281

Exhibition Road

Brompton Road

Harrods

140

24, 465, 428

479

SOUTH
KENSINGTON

59

392
314
242

Sloane Street

104

292 175
45

418

165

*SOUTH
KENSINGTON*

312

461

Eaton Sq

106

470
431

136

7

151

34

5

284

*SLOANE
SQUARE*

141

391

135 361

75

87

109, 162, 433

213

King's Road

730

Chelsea Br Rd

44 →

18

369

CHELSEA

Royal
Hospital

446
128

89

150

346

427

108

196

154

Chelsea Embankment

Cheyne Walk

River Thames

02

Albert Bridge Road

Battersea Bridge Road

Battersea
Park

BATTERSEA

Price Of Wales Drive

Battersea Pk Rd

Map 5 – West (W postcodes)

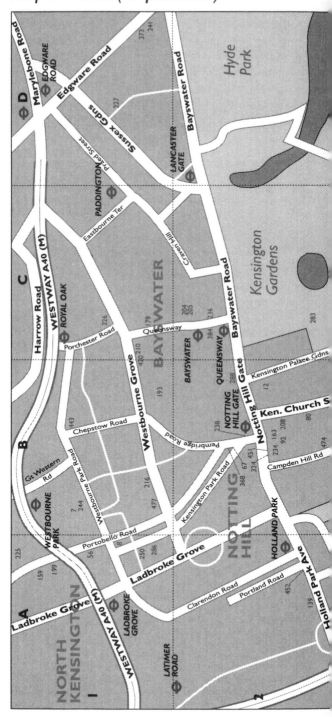

Map 6 – South

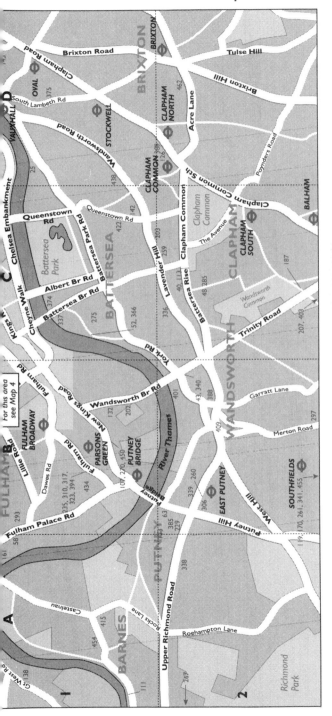

Map 7 – North

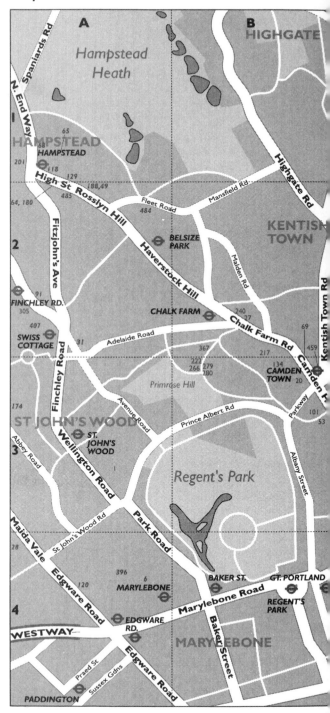

A

B

HIGHGATE

Spaniards Rd

N. End Way

Hampstead Heath

1

HAMPSTEAD

65

HAMPSTEAD

201

118

129

188,49

High St Rosslyn Hill

485

64, 180

Fleet Road

Mansfield Rd

484

Highgate Rd

KENTISH TOWN

Fitzjohn's Ave

2

BELSIZE PARK

Haverstock Hill

Maiden Rd

91

FINCHLEY RD.

305

CHALK FARM

240

27

Kentish Town Rd

407

SWISS COTTAGE

31

Adelaide Road

Chalk Farm Rd

69

459

217

Finchley Road

367

134

CAMDEN TOWN

20

Camden H

222

266 279 280

174

Primrose Hill

ST JOHN'S WOOD

Avenue Road

Prince Albert Rd

Parkway

101

53

3

ST. JOHN'S WOOD

Abbey Road

Wellington Road

I

Regent's Park

Albany Street

Maida Vale

28

Park Road

St John's Wood Rd

396

6

MARYLEBONE

BAKER ST.

GT. PORTLAND

REGENT'S PARK

120

Edgware Road

4

EDGWARE RD.

Marylebone Road

WESTWAY

MARYLEBONE

Baker Street

Edgware Road

Praed St

Sussex Gdns

PADDINGTON

Map 7 – North

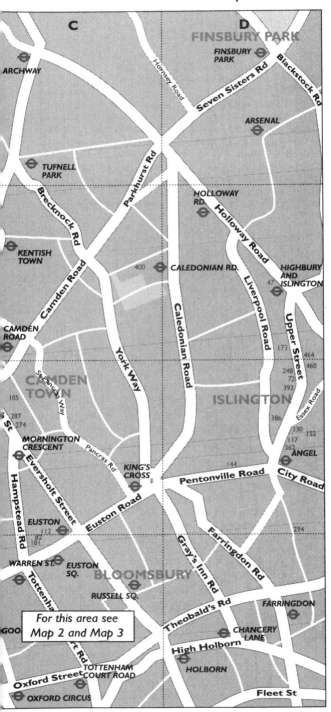

C

D

FINSBURY PARK

FINSBURY PARK

Hornsey Road

Seven Sisters Rd

Blackstock Rd

ARCHWAY

ARSENAL

TUFNELL PARK

Parkhurst Rd

HOLLOWAY RD

Holloway Road

HIGHBURY AND ISLINGTON

Brecknock Rd

47

KENTISH TOWN

400

CALEDONIAN RD.

Liverpool Road

Upper Street

Camden Road

173

CAMDEN ROAD

York Way

Caledonian Road

464
460

St Pancras Way

248
72
393

Essex Road

105

CAMDEN TOWN

ISLINGTON

387
274

386

330   152

St Pancras Way

117

MORNINGTON CRESCENT

Pancras Rd

362

ANGEL

Eversholt Street

KING'S CROSS

144

Hampstead Rd

Pentonville Road

City Road

EUSTON

294

112

Euston Road

87
181

Farringdon Rd

WARREN ST.

EUSTON SQ.

BLOOMSBURY

Gray's Inn Rd

RUSSELL SQ.

FARRINGDON

Tottenha

GOO

For this area see
Map 2 and Map 3

Theobald's Rd

CHANCERY LANE

rt Rd

High Holborn

OXFORD CIRCUS

Oxford Street

TOTTENHAM COURT ROAD

HOLBORN

Fleet St

Map 8 – East (City)

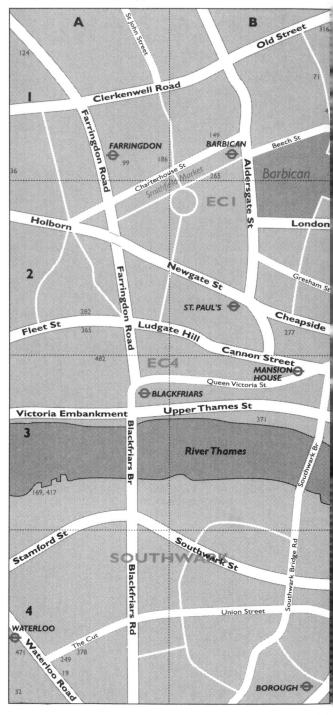

A

St John Street

B

Old Street

316

124

71

4

1

Clerkenwell Road

Farringdon Road

FARRINGDON

149

BARBICAN

Beech St

99

186

Barbican

36

Charterhouse St

Smithfield Market

265

Aldersgate St

EC1

Holborn

London

2

Farringdon Road

Newgate St

Gresham St

ST. PAUL'S

Cheapside

282

Fleet St

365

Ludgate Hill

277

EC4

482

Cannon Street

MANSION HOUSE

Queen Victoria St

BLACKFRIARS

Upper Thames St

Victoria Embankment

371

3

Blackfriars Br

River Thames

Southwark Br

169, 417

Stamford St

Southwark St

Blackfriars Rd

SOUTHWARK

Southwark Bridge Rd

4

Union Street

WATERLOO

471

Waterloo Road

The Cut

249

378

19

BOROUGH

32

Map 8 – East (City)

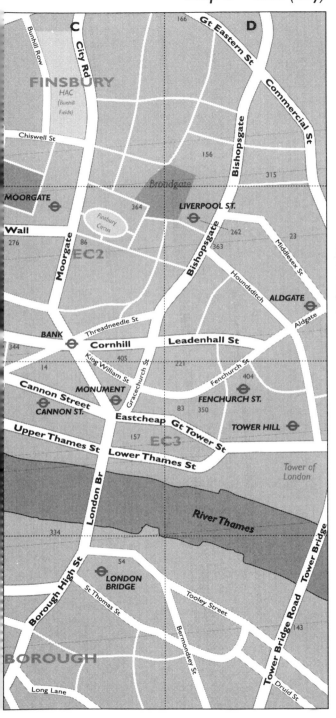

Survey Registration Form

Please complete and return this form if you would like to take part in our annual survey of London restaurants.

(Please note, registration forms received after 21 July 1995 will be recorded for the Summer 1996 survey. We will not disclose your name to any third party.)

Name

Address

Where did you hear about Good Cheap Eats *in London? (If in a shop, please state which.)*

Are there any entries in this guide with which you disagree? If so, which and why?

Is there anywhere you would like to nominate for inclusion in next year's edition?

Do you have any particularly good or bad recent meals to report?

Thank you.
Please send your completed form to:
Harden's Guides
PO Box 1500, London SW5 0DX